THE
FRENCH
WOMEN
DON'T GET FAT
COOKBOOK

the FRENCH WOMEN DON'T GET FAT COOKBOOK

MIREILLE GUILIANO

ATRIA PAPERBACK

NEW YORK   LONDON   TORONTO   SYDNEY

ATRIA PAPERBACK

A Division of Simon & Schuster, Inc.
1230 Avenue of the Americas
New York, NY 10020

First Atria Paperback edition September 2011

ATRIA PAPERBACK and colophon are trademarks of Simon & Schuster, Inc.

French Women Don't Get Fat® is a registered trademark of Mireille Guiliano.

"Magical Leek Soup (Broth)," "Ratatouille," "Pork Chops with Apples," "Grandma Louise's Oatmeal with
Grated Apple," "Duck *à la Gasconne*," "Chicken *au Champagne*" from *French Women Don't Get Fat* by Mireille
Guiliano, copyright © 2005 by Mireille Guiliano. "Leeks Mozzarella," "Sardines with Carrots and Leeks,"
"Mackerel with Carrots and Leeks" from *French Women for All Seasons* by Mireille Guiliano, copyright
© 2006 by Mireille Guiliano. Used by permission of Alfred A. Knopf, a division of Random House, Inc.

For information about special discounts for bulk purchases, please contact
Simon & Schuster Special Sales at 1-866-506-1949 or business@simonandschuster.com.

The Simon & Schuster Speakers Bureau can bring authors to your live event. For
more information or to book an event, contact the Simon & Schuster Speakers Bureau
at 1-866-248-3049 or visit our website at www.simonspeakers.com.

Designed by Jaime Putorti

Manufactured in the United States of America

10   9   8   7   6   5

The Library of Congress has cataloged the hardcover edition as follows:

Guiliano, Mireille, date.
   The French women don't get fat cookbook / Mireille Guiliano.
     p. cm.
Includes index.
   1. Reducing diets—Recipes. 2. Women—Health and hygiene—France. 3. Cookery,
French. I. Title.
   RM222.2.G7853 2010
   641.5'635—dc22

                   2009041646

ISBN 978-1-4391-4896-9
ISBN 978-1-4391-4897-6 (pbk)
ISBN 978-1-4391-9933-6 (ebook)

CONTENTS

Ouverture   *1*

1. Breakfast and *Le Brunch*   7

2. Sometimes It Is Called Lunch   59

3. Dinner *à Table*   107

4. Eat Your Fish and Vegetables   151

5. Closures—Sweet, Chocolate, and Otherwise   179

6. Putting It All Together   207

7. Once in a While a Little Champagne   241

8. In Case You Were About to Ask   263

Cuisiner dans la Cuisine, or Cooking in the Kitchen   *285*

Remerciements   *289*

Index   *291*

....

A FEW WORDS BEFORE WE EAT

There's a line in my biography that always gets a laugh when I am introduced: "Her favorite pastimes are breakfast, lunch, and dinner." It's all true—people always laugh, and I do take enormous pleasure in and shape my life around meals.

I remember introducing my husband, Edward, to my family in France, an orientation that mostly took place around meals. The smell of a freshly baked breakfast cake would lure him into the kitchen where he'd wake up with some freshly squeezed orange juice (something more American than French, but freshly squeezed to be sure in my parents' house), then a little protein in the form of eggs or cheese or yogurt to go along with the cake and fresh coffee.

Nothing extensive or elaborate, but a healthy start to the day for certain. Before he left the breakfast table my mother would be talking about and preparing lunch, the main meal of the day. It didn't take him long to observe, "You know, your family is always either eating or talking about food." True enough.

Some years later during one of those lunches with my family he asked coyly, "Might it be possible to eat and enjoy this meal before talking about and planning the next one?" It seems we had mastered the art that he had not of enjoying the present while anticipating with all our senses what was to come. That certainly is a French trait. For years now when he and I are in restaurants in France and overhear people enjoying their meal while frequently recounting recent or anticipated meals in other restaurants or sharing recipes and food stories, we give each other a knowing look and shrug.

Yes, breakfast, lunch, and dinner are my favorite pastimes, and that is how I have mostly organized this book of recipes and stories. But the lines of demarcation can be blurry. Some of the same dishes in different portion sizes can be served as the day's main meal, which we normally call dinner, or at the less substantial meal we call lunch if it comes at midday.

I grew up eating my main meal at midday, so is that lunch or dinner? Well, in many areas and throughout much of history, it has been and is called both. Then the last meal of the day is lighter and akin to lunch and is called supper, in part attributable to the French verb *souper,* which relates to soup, common evening fare after a big meal at midday.

And who says you can't have scrambled eggs now and again for dinner . . . at night? So, whether I am offering soups or salads, fish or meat, pasta or vegetables, the recipes that follow are available and inviting for your own *mix-and-match*. In organizing this book I have purposely chosen *not* to always follow conventional logic or be sequential and Cartesian in presenting all the chicken dishes in one spot or all the pasta dishes in another. I've broken these recipes down into three meals, but the rest of the choice is up to you. If you prefer to have your biggest meal midday, feel free to skim the dinner chapter for your lunchtime meal. (Who could argue with pasta for lunch? I've even been known to eat oatmeal at night!)

Of course, I am not suggesting pasta dishes for lunch and again for dinner. I enjoy reading recipes almost every day of my life. For me, reading a single recipe is an intellectual act. For each preparation of, say, chicken, I play it consciously and unconsciously against all the chicken recipes I know, have prepared, or have eaten. I see them—I taste them. I might think this one is like grandma's chicken in a pot, but with x, y, and z added or different. I can taste the differences the way a musician can play a tune in her head from sheet music. (I don't think that's a particularly uncommon trait for anyone who cooks.) And I wish you the mental pleasures of experiencing the recipes presented here in the order that they appear, or in whatever order you wish.

I believe it is important to eat three times a day, to eat in moderation, and to enjoy balanced meals that include protein, fat, and carbohydrates. That's how I live. Breakfast is perhaps the most important meal, and, as simple as it sounds, supplies the fuel for the early stages of the day. In my experience, the people who "don't eat breakfast," or "just have a cup of coffee," are the same ones eating fattening food, primarily carbohydrates, at their desks or in their kitchens at 11 o'clock. Or because they are dehydrated and hungry, they drink soda as a pick-me-up. And if they get so caught up in a meeting or conference call or whatever and make it to lunch without eating, then, of course, they overdo it. Two or three slices of pizza at lunch isn't the stuff of people who know what they are putting in their body. If any of this rings a bell, don't despair: I promise it is possible to eat for pleasure and modify one's eating patterns. And this book provides what I hope are many tempting meal choices.

So, here's a reminder: eat breakfast. And do not overdose on sugar as a morning stimulant by having oversize portions of fruit juice, sugar-laced cereals, breads, and pastries. Bagels and donuts are indulgences, not the core ingredients of a healthy daily meal. With a healthy breakfast, it is possible, if you choose, to have a very modest lunch—but eat something, say some nuts, fruit, yogurt, a soup or salad (half a sandwich? But what to do with the other half?)—rather than pass on lunch altogether, which results in a parallel unhealthy practice of afternoon snacking and/or overdoing it at dinner. "I only eat one big meal a day" is not a motto to live by or be proud of.

Recipes are a personal photo album, a chronicle of who you were and who you are today. My recipes obviously reflect my childhood in France, my adult life in New York and France, and my extensive travels and meals for business and pleasure around America and the world. But mostly they reflect a series of principles on eating for pleasure that I have learned over the years and shared in my two French Women books and on my websites. Almost all are published here in my own interpretations of dishes I've enjoyed with family or friends or "inventions" for the first time. For a little added balance, I include a small selection of a few classic dishes revisited, plus a handful of recipes from my two French Women books that readers have enjoyed.

My philosophy isn't about "dieting" in the conventional sense, but more about eating sensibly and pleasurably. It is partly a cry—okay, more like a whimper—for sanity in an increasingly developed world where, ironically, the abundance of food has become a challenge to good health. Cultural and religious differences as well as the local availability of foodstuffs historically have been the greatest drivers of what we put on our plates, but globalization has meant eating the same genetically modified fruits and vegetables the world over, seasons without end, and spending much less time in the kitchen cooking. As we all recognize, prepared foods, fast food, junk foods abound and people can become overwhelmed by choices (even with yogurts, apples, cheeses, and on and on) and lose touch with what they are putting in their bodies. Cooking is a reality check. Beyond reiterating, expanding, and illustrating the principles that guide my eating and have enabled me to enjoy food and maintain balance and a healthy, consistent weight, I propose to offer—as many of my readers have asked—more meals and recipes that are easy, quick, affordable, and delicious—minimum effort and stress for maximum results.

Yes, I believe in pure and simple recipes. Once in a while I enjoy long hours in the kitchen, but mostly a half hour or even less is enough to put three colors of food on a main plate. (Even my mother's braising and slow cooking required little work once the flame was on—the stove did all the work.)

I like to taste the pure flavors of those balanced ingredients. To me that means buying quality ingredients, which often results in small portions yielding high satisfaction. So, I advise working with foods that taste as good as they look if you want the maximum of pleasure. No matter how great the recipe, tired or tasteless vegetables yield tired or tasteless dishes. And there is no significant correlation between generally tasty and healthy vegetables (or other well-chosen foods) and price. Lots of great things to eat are relatively inexpensive. Work with them.

I like variety in what I eat. Eating fresh foods in season can facilitate this, as well as judicious selection from the freezer section of the supermarket. On the one hand, I like recipes that force good portion control, and on the other, I like it when one preparation can become two meals through a later use of some previously cooked items. So leftovers are for me additional pleasures, and are also in tune with French women's sense of frugality and *débrouillardise* (resourcefulness). I like recipes that work, and all of the recipes in this book have been tested multiple times and on different stoves, since ovens vary according to the changes in the weather and the localized character of the ingredients, such as milk, butter, oil, and the foods themselves. But recipes are guides not laws, so play with them to suit your tastes and kitchen. And most of the recipes I present, for reasons of efficiency, economy, and consistency, serve four. If you are cooking for one, two, or eight, in most cases you should be able to interpolate without a loss in quality. And always have fun.

I especially like recipes that make a meal a sensual experience in that it speaks to all five of our senses—from the look to the texture to the smell and taste, though I confess sound is the least compelling. Of course, recipes need to yield food that tastes good. It is all about pleasures and good health, you'll see.

Chapter One

BREAKFAST
AND *LE BRUNCH*

I confess my greatest culinary transformation in life concerns breakfast, and my approach to it continues to evolve. I eat breakfast religiously and, I believe, healthily. That wasn't always the case. Growing up in France, I ate a light breakfast (remember we had our main meal at midday, sometimes not long after I awoke, so I was not always looking to fill up). Generally my breakfast consisted of carbohydrates and coffee. A cup of café au lait and perhaps a piece of bread with butter and preserves (my mother's own). Or a slice of the breakfast cake my mother would make once or twice a week. Once in a while, I ate stale bread in chunks in a *bol*, like a soup bowl, softened and moistened with a soup-size portion of coffee and milk. No protein, no fruit. I was not alone in France. A croissant and coffee, anyone?

Things did not improve when I came to America as an exchange student. Mostly carbohydrates and coffee again. Once in a while I ingested an egg or two, but with bacon and sometimes potatoes. But those carbs—I discovered donuts and bagels, two of which many consider the most delicious albeit fattening and unhealthy foods on earth. Moderation? I only ate one bagel. Who knew that a bagel is loaded with salt and contains as many calories/carbs as a few slices of bread? But, of course, I covered my bagel with cream cheese and jam. Being French, more jam than cream cheese, so I was getting very little protein. And have you noticed the super-sizing of bagels? Not if you were born in the past quarter century. Before that, they actually were what we mostly call mini-bagels today. Plus, being French, I was not then nor am I now into getting my protein or water from a glass of milk. Donuts are deep-fried, and I did not restrict myself to just one. The most wonderful discovery of all was muffins, English muffins and blueberry muffins. Who knew? At least they are not fried. I was also introduced to dry cereal in a bowl covered with milk and perhaps with an added banana. And then there was orange juice in a cardboard carton and served in an eight-ounce water glass. But perhaps most memorable of all was that special occasion breakfast: pancakes. Living in New England, I developed a lifelong fondness for maple syrup. No question, I enjoyed and enjoy all of the above, but now in moderation and balance, or better as occasional indulgences.

When I returned to Paris for college, the now plump me drank coffee as my morning stimulant and ate pastry for breakfast (and lunch . . . and dinner). But I lived to tell the tale (in book form). I remember from then through my twenties dismissing German, Scandinavian, even English breakfasts as unappetizing and huge. I wasn't going to eat meat or fish or eggs and cheese and get fat (again). Sausages for breakfast? Please . . .

I am still not a fan of big breakfasts, but am a devotee of and convert to balanced breakfasts (and lunch and dinner): some protein, some carbohydrates, some fat (a holy trinity of sorts), and fluids. I often do eat a slice (or slivers) of cheese. And, I consider breakfast the most important meal of the day. Don't skip it or your wheels tend to come off in a hurry. My true breakfast epiphany occurred just a few years ago when one day a family breakfast specialty, perfected by *Tante* Berthe, and one that I had not thought about or eaten since childhood burst upon my inner eye and palate and changed everything.

Magical Breakfast Cream (with no cream) or MBC

Here's one of my secrets, really *Tante* Berthe's, for some quick and healthy weight loss without dieting. Aunt Berthe had her slow but sure way to lose ten pounds effortlessly each summer. So while most of the French families I knew when I was growing up (and it's still true today) indulged on vacation and came back with a few extra pounds, she came back svelte and *bien dans sa peau*.

I adored my *Tante* Berthe. One of five sisters, she was *Grand-mère* Louise's youngest sister, and although all of the sisters were attractive women with similar features, blue or green eyes, great cheekbones, long hair kept in gorgeous chignons (I used to love to watch Aunt Berthe do her hair), beautiful peachy skin, and a small nose ever so slightly *retroussé*, *Tante* Berthe had that little extra *je ne sais quoi*. Maybe it was her small round glasses or her beautiful smile or her mischievous look that showed in her sparkling eyes. She was also funny, had a great laugh, and sang beautifully while cooking. She always dressed simply with a gray or navy blue long skirt and had the most seductive tops from lovely classic blouses to *charmeuses* in soft cotton, pale colors, and lace, and only a few pieces of classic jewelry. And she loved hats. She was the only sister living by herself, and her status was never discussed although we knew she was not a *veuve* (a widow) since she was addressed as Madame Berthe Juncker. (In France had she been a widow she would have been referred to as Madame Veuve Juncker, like Madame Veuve Clicquot, a famous "widow" from Champagne.) We knew she had some beau, at least we grasped some of that among relatives' hushed conversations. She seemed to have enough money to live without working though she lived rather frugally and would spend the year visiting relatives to help out with children and cooking usually for a week or two at a time and then move on, either go back to her home or travel (some would say disappear) for a week or so. She was also the most gourmande and gourmet and tended to get a bit pleasantly plump particularly at the end of the winter fêtes, but at the end of each summer she was at her best and looked like a movie star. No one could figure out what she had done: Grandma Louise alone knew but surely kept the secret, and we kids had no idea what the secret was and certainly made no connection with her magical breakfast.

She was the favorite aunt of all the grandchildren: Some adults in the family (especially the men) would say because she was the best cook and an incomparable baker; some said because she was single and spoiling us to no end (and she did). I was her very favorite and as such had an added privilege. When she was in town—she lived in Metz—I could visit her once a month on Thursday, the off school day at the time, and believe me I never missed a day between my seventh and twelfth birthdays (before boys started replacing her on my priority list). I would proudly take the one-hour local bus ride by myself (a conversation piece in my town), and she'd be waiting for me at the bus station. Our day together would always start with me going across the street from the station to try the escalator in the Prisunic, a small department store, a novelty I could brag about with my school friends who had never tried or seen one. She would patiently wait as she was scared of that thing. (It is a quaint reminder that there is a first time for everything, and for a seven-year-old in France, where even today escalators are far rarer than in America, an escalator can be an amusement.) After I had gone up and down a few times on the escalator with a great smile on my face, she'd give me signs indicating it was time for lunch at her house. She lived about a ten-minute walk from the store and station, and we could reach her home via an enchanting road along the Moselle River. She had a wonderful little flat, a lovely terrace with a glass-top awning, and wisteria vines. The terrace overlooked residential homes surrounded with gardens. It was country within the city.

Once there, she'd make my favorite lunch, hanger steak with French fries. (You gather by now that she made the best French fries in the world, even better than my mom, and I alone knew her secret; her trick was to make batches in a small, heavy cocotte versus using the typical large deep fryer.) Dessert would always be a seasonal surprise. I loved her for all this. I did not fancy her magical breakfast then or when we were all in the country for the summer. I realize now it was because when she was with us during her week of magical breakfast cream (a week a month, for the two summer months) we would be deprived of the aroma of fresh brioche, *pain aux raisins,* morning cakes, or fruit tarts baking in the wooden stove and perfuming the whole house and the back garden where breakfast would be served. And for a whole week! We couldn't stand it. Complaining and bickering did nothing. She ignored us. We never even noticed that no wine was served during that week. Continued whining didn't change a thing, there was nothing we could do or say to make her change that pattern. Reluctantly, we got used to it and made silly jokes about it. When the regular routine was resumed, she only nibbled at all the goodies but did so discreetly, so that it too went unnoticed. Smart lady.

My recent epiphany and how this episode of my childhood I had sort of forgotten about returned via an early morning telephone call one spring morning while I was working on my business book. Coralie, an old friend's daughter from Eastern France, was telling me how her mother was making my aunt's summer breakfast. Wow. I had not thought of it in decades and thus never made it but instantly visualized the village farmhouse, our summer vacation in a lovely small village near Strasbourg, and the magical mornings eating the summer breakfast in the back of the house watching the fawns come near us (did they like the smell of my aunt's breakfasts?), hearing her grind the nuts and cereal in her mortar and add it to her homemade yogurt base made alternatively from cow, sheep, or goat milk. So, I searched in my recipe boxes and there it was scribbled on a small yellowish piece of disintegrating paper, my *Tante* Berthe's version.

Here's our "family" version that my aunt would make. Beware: it is addictive. It's also extremely easy and quick to make, and one can play and interchange so many ingredients. It is the perfect complete breakfast and will keep you from getting hungry until late lunch. You may have run across Johanna Budwig's variation. A German chemist, pharmacologist, and physicist who lived during much of the twentieth century (and came after my aunt), she promoted a version using cottage cheese as a cancer-fighting breakfast and also part of a nutrition plan. I've made MBC in quite a few versions and can't decide which is my favorite, as it is all a function of where I am, what I feel like, and with whom I share it.

Why do I call it magical breakfast cream? Magical? Something that is a combination of tasty, easy, and so good for your well-being and melts away pounds has to be magical, right? How many pounds? Try a week of MBC for breakfast with a normal but modest lunch and dinner (soup or salad, fish, two vegetables, and fruit), and say good-bye effortlessly to a few pounds, if dozens of converts reporting back from my website are any indication. The trick here is to eat MBC and also to cut two offenders (for me it's bread and wine) and otherwise eat normally. It works splendidly, and your energy and well-being after these few days are remarkable.

Cream, you may ask? There is no cream in it, but the texture looks like cream and cream connotes something utterly sensual such as comfort food and pampering—except in this case you need not worry about the calories. I trust my aunt used the word to make sure we kids would love it and never mentioned the *oil* in the mixture. Smart lady again: no one can taste the oil anyway. That oil, by the way, is preferably flaxseed oil, a superconcentrated source of omega-3 fatty acid that has so many health benefits.

In a variation on a theme dear to me, and a paraphrase of a quote from Lily Bollinger on Champagne, let me say: "I eat it when I am happy and when I am sad. I eat it when I am alone and consider it obligatory when I have company. I trifle with it when I am not hungry and always eat it when I am."

Have fun playing with the range of options and make your own version. Remember, it's like fashion: mix and match to please your own taste buds.

MAGICAL BREAKFAST CREAM

• SERVES 1 •

4 to 6 tablespoons yogurt
(about ½ cup)

1 teaspoon flaxseed oil

1 to 2 tablespoons lemon
juice (Meyer or organic
preferably)

1 teaspoon honey

2 tablespoons finely ground
cereal (with zero sugar
such as Post Shredded
Wheat)

2 teaspoons finely ground
walnuts

1. Put the yogurt in a bowl and add the oil. Mix well. Add the lemon juice and mix well. Add the honey and mix well. (It is important to add each ingredient one at a time and mix well to obtain a homogeneous preparation.)

2. Finely grind the cereal and walnuts (I use a small food processor). Add to the yogurt mixture and mix well. Serve at once.

TIME-SAVER: *You can do a week's worth of grinding cereal/nuts mixture and keep it refrigerated so in the morning it will take just a few instants to mix the yogurt with the oil (have no fear, you will not taste the oil in the final creamy blend), add the lemon juice, honey, and your daily dose of cereal/nut mixture—et voilà.*

NOTE: *I use Post Shredded Wheat Original made from whole grain wheat, adding to this recipe a "health-friendly" mix of 0 grams sugar, 0 grams sodium, and 6 grams of fiber per cup (and I use only 2 tablespoons per serving).*

You can replace the yogurt with ricotta, cottage cheese (beware of high sodium content), *fromage blanc,* or should you be in France, try it with *faisselle.* When using yogurt you can opt for whole or 2% milk. I make my own yogurt and do not like skim milk, which tastes like water to me.

You can replace the flaxseed oil with sesame oil or safflower oil.

You can replace the lemon juice with grapefruit juice, orange juice, or blood orange juice. With orange juice, use less honey.

You can replace the honey with maple syrup. As the latter is less sweet than honey, you may want to adjust to your taste.

You can replace the shredded wheat with buckwheat, barley, oatmeal, or any cereal that contains no sugar, a key in this recipe.

You can replace the walnuts with hazelnuts, almonds, or a mixture of both. Pecans, pine nuts, and any other nuts work fine, too.

Finally, you can adjust the doses of the juice (I tend to add more lemon juice when using something thicker than yogurt and because I love it) and the honey (less rather than more). My husband chooses 2 tablespoons of fresh orange juice, which is sweet enough and in his case requires nothing else to compensate for honey, although some times (on Sundays!) he'll add a drizzle of maple syrup (my theory being it is his make-believe for not having pancakes or waffles! Why not?).

You can also add fruit: the obvious is half of a ripe banana mashed with a fork and added after step one or sliced and placed on top of the finished dish. Or top it with any seasonal fruit, especially a mix of berries in summer or dried cranberries, raisins, dried fig or date pieces, or even diced prunes in the cold months. Try it plain, though, as it is simply delicious and in its purest form. And, as recommended, create your own versions. And a last recommendation: surprise your kids with your favorite concoction as in a blind wine tasting—no details on what it is until after the first taste and a little riddle.

Giovanna, a Roman friend in her early thirties who is nuts about food, particularly French food (don't we always want what we don't have, as so many of us, French and American women, love Italian food?), is someone I have had great meals with at home and in restaurants in Italy, France, and in the United States, mostly New York City. She loves to cook for her family and friends, and during our cooking sessions, we've spent time comparing recipes, making new dishes, and learning from each other when it comes to the presentation of food. We've had lots of laughs in the kitchen and at the table talking about food and wine and making fun of each other's culture and rituals.

She admitted that though she's never had a weight problem and is a tall, pretty young woman, she had applied a few things from my books that she didn't know about or had not yet incorporated in her eating plan, and her body was transformed. She had not really lost weight, well, maybe two to three pounds, but looks like *une belle plante* (a flattering expression French men use when they see a gorgeous woman) and was glad that I said I had noticed . . .

When she stayed with me in Provence, I introduced her to the MBC. I sincerely do not believe I had ever seen anyone enjoy something so simple so much. Eating it, she was *miam miaming* (yum yumming) like a baby. And from then on, we had the MBC every morning. Then she went home and started experimenting. She is not as crazy as I am about lemons (too acidic), so she experimented with orange juice. Here's her latest, and I must say *très réussie* (well done), an Italian interpretation of *Tante* Berthe's basic recipe:

GIOVANNA'S MBC

• SERVES 1 •

½ cup 2% plain Greek-style yogurt

1 teaspoon flaxseed oil

1 tablespoon finely ground nuts (equal parts walnuts, hazelnuts, and almonds)

1 teaspoon honey

2 tablespoons finely ground old-fashioned oatmeal

Juice and pulp of 2 clementines or tangerines (only available for a couple of winter months) or ½ orange (not quite as delicate)

1. Put the yogurt and flaxseed oil in a cereal bowl and mix well.

2. Add the ground nuts and honey and mix.

3. Add the ground oats on the surface, but don't mix yet. Pour the juice and pulp over and leave for a few seconds, then mix and taste.

And here is her reasoning for her improved version, her treaty on *cuisine moléculaire*! "The small amount of fat in the 2% yogurt is a plus. [We agree on that one.] Oats have fiber and starch, which even in the uncooked version, once in contact with acid substances (citrus food), are practically predigested, and this explains why I prefer to leave the juice on it to be in contact with the oats before mixing it. The acidity level of the clementines is well tolerated by the surface of my teeth and my stomach. Furthermore, for one who loves sugar, it's the type of citrus fruit that is the most delicate; thus when I press the juice, I am careful to pick up any pulp left on the juicer, and so all those little fibers stay in the 'cream,' which is truly fresh, light, thirst quenching, and extra *gourmande*—at least for my taste buds." And apparently my aunt's, too.

And now Giovanna has converted her mother and even her grandmother, who professed not to like yogurt. Here's the account: Giovanna wrote she missed her MBC (due to a rushed day visiting relatives), but made it for a snack in the afternoon while visiting her grandmother. "I made my grandmother taste it, not telling her anything about the ingredients, as she has repeatedly stated to all family members she does not like yogurt and makes disgusted facial expressions when she mentions the word. Here is the surprise: She loved it (my mother was present, knew the ingredients, and was quietly smiling) and looked like a *bébé gourmand*, eating teaspoon after teaspoon to the point when I had to ask whether I should make more or would she leave me some." She finished hers. Imagine if she had liked yogurt!

Eggs

Happy days now that eggs are back in favor—thank you, thank you—not only because they are tasty but because in moderation they are very good for you due to their exceptional nutritional qualities. The egg is actually a small dietetic miracle possessing vitamins A, B, D, E, and K, minerals (notably iron and phosphorus), as well as selenium and iodine. And it's now, *enfin*, confirmed that three eggs a week have no effect on cholesterol (three quarters of which is made by the body itself anyway), since egg is perfectly digestible and well tolerated by our liver. Eggs being a good source of proteins, they are a nice alternative to meat, especially as our body absorbs their nutrients quite easily. As wonderful as the French breakfast of coffee, croissant, and brioche is, (wo)man cannot live by bread alone. How about a little protein added with a yogurt or egg dish?

When I was a student in Weston, Massachusetts, and lived with six very different families during the school year, I was introduced to sunny-side-up eggs (I love the expression, which reminds me of sunflowers) and bacon. One thing these six families shared was fried eggs for breakfast—at some households it was on the breakfast menu three to five times a week. The men in the family would eat three eggs and I dare not remember or mention how many slices of bacon. *Oh la la.* What a shock that was. First, because we never had eggs for breakfast in my family (but ate our dose in prepared salted or sweet dishes). Yet we had omelets (filled with whatever was in season from mushrooms to asparagus or simply cheese and herbs if there was nothing else in the fridge), but usually for unexpected guests at dinner or some light dinners a couple of times a month, especially on weekends after a multicourse long lunch. Once a week as children we were allowed one *oeuf à la coque,* the soft-boiled egg served in one of *Mamie*'s prize collection of *coquetiers* (eggcups) with *mouillettes,* the little sticks of bread cut into slim rectangles and just toasted, the ones French kids grow up with and the perfect accessory to "wet" the egg yolk with, since it was not proper to let the yolk leak out—it was all in the art of handling the *mouil-*

lette. I came to realize that French and Americans both eat plenty of eggs, just differently.

My reasons for liking eggs go beyond their vitamins and minerals, which make them a great food for any age group. They are inexpensive and keep for a couple of weeks in the fridge, though I'd recommend taking them out 20 minutes before cooking. They are light, easy to digest, and good at any meal and a quick way to make a meal (3 minutes for a soft-boiled egg, a few more for an omelet). Hard-boiled eggs are perfect for an *en cas* (emergency food, in case) or a picnic (I often bring one on the plane for dinner or breakfast on overnight flights, one never knows). They are a savior for last-minute guests (make sure to always have some cheese in your fridge) showing up hungry. They are also and foremost delicious in desserts from sweet omelets to French toast, floating island, and the almighty *crème anglaise* not to mention custard, puddings, and soufflés. The textural differences and pleasures one can achieve with eggs are endless.

My houseguests in Provence always tease me when I announce an "English breakfast," which is basically one or two eggs any style, toasted baguette, some local jam, yogurt, a portion of fruit, and a nice cup (or two) of coffee or tea, mixed with a surprise or two like a tomato salad (eh, we are in Provence after all) or a polenta dish for those who want to eat out of the box. Sitting on the terrace and enjoying the first song of the day from our friends the *cigales,* life does not get any better. And the proof is that people linger, relax, converse, and don't want to leave the table; sometimes they stay there until we announce lunch. Maybe my travel to many parts of the world also influenced my way of reassessing breakfast and playing not only with variety but completeness. I'm not up to serving a Chinese breakfast in Manhattan or a Japanese one in Provence, but I like to play on the "when in Rome" dictum, and I love dishes and flavors my guests do and I let them compose their own magical treat. The trick is not to go to the extreme and gorge oneself but carefully pick à la carte. So, generally I pick one of the following recipes for the "staple" breakfast dish.

SOFT SCRAMBLED EGGS

· SERVES 6 TO 8 ·

12 eggs

2 tablespoons butter, cut
   into small pieces

¼ teaspoon salt

2 tablespoons heavy cream

1. Fill a saucepan with 1 inch of water, place over medium-high heat, and bring to a simmer.

2. Break the eggs into a double boiler insert and place on top of a simmering water bath. Add the butter and salt and cook, whisking constantly, until the eggs thicken, small curds form, and they become very creamy, 5 to 6 minutes.

3. Immediately remove from the heat and stir in the cream, which will stop the cooking process and make the eggs even creamier. Serve immediately.

PROVENÇAL OMELET

· SERVES 4 ·

3 teaspoons olive oil

3 teaspoons unsalted butter

¼ cup peeled and minced shallots

½ cup white mushrooms, cleaned and sliced

1 teaspoon lemon juice

¼ cup broccoli florets, cut into ½-inch pieces

½ yellow pepper, cut into strips

Salt and freshly ground pepper

10 eggs

½ cup grated Gruyère

½ cup grated Parmesan

1 tomato, rinsed and diced

1 cup baby spinach

½ cup fresh basil leaves cut into chiffonade (thin strips)

Baguette for serving

1. Heat 1 teaspoon of the olive oil and 1 teaspoon of the butter in a medium (9-inch) nonstick skillet over medium heat. Add the shallots and sauté until softened, about 2 minutes. Add the mushrooms, lemon juice, and broccoli and sauté for 2 minutes. Add the yellow pepper and sauté for an additional 2 minutes until crisp-tender. Remove the vegetables from the pan, season to taste, and reserve.

2. In a large bowl, whisk the eggs and season to taste. Heat 1 teaspoon oil and 1 teaspoon butter over medium-high heat in the same skillet. Add half of the eggs to the pan and shake the pan a bit, lifting the edges of the omelet up to allow the uncooked egg to run underneath. Cook until the top is just set, about 1 minute. Sprinkle the eggs with half of the grated cheeses and place half of the sautéed vegetables, tomato, and spinach on one side of the omelet. Using a large spatula, fold the other side of the omelet over to cover the vegetable filling and allow to cook for 1 minute. Carefully slide onto a platter and repeat with the remaining ingredients for the other omelet.

3. To serve, place both omelets on a platter and garnish with fresh basil. Serve immediately with slices of a baguette.

TRICOLOR OMELET

• SERVES 4 •

3 tablespoons plus 1 teaspoon unsalted butter

3 large shallots, peeled and finely chopped

10 eggs

Salt and freshly ground pepper

2 tablespoons each finely chopped fresh parsley, basil, and thyme

1 medium tomato, cut into ¼-inch dice

1. Melt 1 teaspoon butter in a small nonstick sauté pan over medium heat. Add the shallots and sauté until softened. Remove the pan from the heat and cool.

2. In a large bowl, whisk the eggs together and season to taste. Divide the eggs among three bowls: in the first bowl, add the herbs, in the second, tomato, and in the third, shallots. Stir each mixture and season with salt and pepper.

3. Melt 1 tablespoon butter in the pan used for the shallots over medium-high heat. Add the egg-herb mixture to the pan, tilting and swirling the pan to evenly distribute the egg mixture. When the top is set, carefully flip the mixture over and cook for another minute. Slide onto a plate and keep warm.

4. Repeat with the remaining two egg mixtures to make three omelets, stacking the cooked omelets on top of one another. Garnish with additional herbs if desired, and serve immediately, cut into wedges.

FRIED EGGS, SPANISH STYLE

• SERVES 4 •

20 thin slices chorizo

2 tablespoons olive oil

1 large shallot, peeled and
   sliced

4 eggs

Salt and freshly ground
   pepper

1. Preheat the oven to 400 degrees.

2. Place the chorizo on a small baking sheet and cook in the oven for 1 to 2 minutes. Remove from the oven and transfer the slices to a paper towel–lined plate to drain. Reserve.

3. Heat the oil in a medium nonstick frying pan over medium-low heat. Add the shallot and sauté for 3 minutes to infuse the oil. Remove the shallot from the pan and discard. Break 2 eggs into the pan and cook for 1 minute. Baste the eggs with the shallot-infused oil and cook for another minute or until set. Carefully remove the eggs from the pan and place on a paper towel–lined plate to drain and keep warm. Repeat with the remaining 2 eggs.

4. To serve, place 1 egg on a warmed plate, season to taste, and garnish with the warm chorizo slices.

POACHED EGGS WITH SALMON AND SPINACH

1 teaspoon peeled and
   minced shallot

1 teaspoon lemon zest

1 tablespoon lemon juice

2 tablespoons olive oil

Salt and freshly ground
   pepper

2 cups spinach

½ cup shaved fennel (about
   ½ small fennel bulb)

1 tablespoon white wine
   vinegar

4 eggs

4 ounces thinly sliced
   smoked salmon

Baguette for serving

1. In a small bowl, whisk together the shallot, lemon zest, lemon juice, and olive oil and season to taste. Place the spinach and fennel in a bowl, add the dressing, and toss well to combine. Set aside.

2. Fill a 10- to 12-inch skillet with 2½ inches water, add the vinegar, and bring to a simmer over medium-high heat. Break each egg into a small cup and add to the water one at a time. Cook the eggs until the whites are just set, about 1½ minutes. Carefully remove the eggs with a slotted spoon.

3. To serve, place one slice of salmon on each plate. Top with a portion of spinach salad and a poached egg. Season to taste and serve immediately with slices of a baguette.

HAM AND LEEK FRITTATA

• SERVES 4 •

6 eggs

1 teaspoon grainy mustard

Pinch of red pepper flakes

Salt and freshly ground
    pepper

2 tablespoons unsalted
    butter

1 tablespoon olive oil

1 leek, white part only,
    rinsed and thinly sliced

4 ounces baked ham, cut
    into small pieces

1. Preheat the broiler.

2. In a medium bowl, whisk together the eggs, mustard, and pepper flakes and season with salt and pepper.

3. Heat the butter and olive oil in a large nonstick oven-safe skillet over medium heat until the butter has melted. Add the leek and cook, stirring, until softened, 3 to 4 minutes. Add the ham and cook, stirring, until warm, about 2 minutes.

4. Add the egg mixture and swirl the skillet to distribute the eggs and filling evenly over the surface. Shake the skillet gently, tilting slightly while lifting the edges of the frittata with a spatula to let the raw egg run underneath for the first 1 to 2 minutes. Cook until the eggs are almost set, about 5 minutes total, and place the skillet under the broiler (not too close) for 1 minute. The frittata will puff up and brown slightly. Remove from the oven and carefully slide the frittata out of the skillet using a spatula. Cut into wedges and serve hot, at room temperature, or cold.

NOTE: *If desired, sprinkle ½ cup grated Gruyère on top of the frittata just before placing under the broiler.*

ZUCCHINI AND FRESH GOAT CHEESE FRITTATA

• SERVES 4 •

6 eggs

1½ small unpeeled zucchini, rinsed and grated (about 1 cup)

2 tablespoons fresh thyme (or chopped marjoram)

4 ounces fresh goat cheese (or feta), crumbled

Salt and freshly ground pepper

1 tablespoon olive oil

⅓ cup grated pecorino

1 small sprig fresh thyme

1. Preheat the broiler.

2. Break the eggs into a bowl and beat slightly with a fork. Add the zucchini, thyme, and goat cheese, stir to combine, and season to taste.

3. Heat the olive oil in a large, nonstick, oven-safe skillet over medium-high heat. Add the egg mixture and swirl the pan to distribute the eggs and filling evenly over the surface. Shake the pan gently, tilting slightly while lifting the edges of the frittata with a spatula to let the egg run underneath for the first 1 to 2 minutes. Lower the heat to medium and cook until the eggs are almost set, 5 to 7 minutes.

4. Cover the frittata with the pecorino and place the pan under the broiler (not too close) for 1 minute. The frittata will puff up and brown slightly and the cheese will melt. Remove from the oven, garnish with the thyme, and serve.

Comfort Food

I don't know when I first heard the term comfort food; it probably was only in the last decade, but it hit home immediately. Comfort foods are those security blanket dishes that evoke childhood memories and a sense of well-being. They are extremely cultural as well—from macaroni and cheese to steak and mashed potatoes for some New Yorkers. With the Alsatian cultural influence in my family, desserts rise to the comfort food class from cakes with raisins, ginger, nutmeg, and lots of cinnamon to cookies with anise seeds to sugar tarts with more cinnamon, but also all types of custards—flans and puddings with berries in syrup and fresh fruit tarts being the ultimate, especially those on the sour side with *groseilles* (red currants), *griottes* (a bitter type of cherries), *quetsches* (like some Italian plums), and rhubarb, not everyone's cup of tea but a wonderful reminder of the aroma in the kitchen at baking time.

Can pickles and seaweed be comfort foods for breakfast? Who eats pickles and seaweed for breakfast in the first place? That's right, the Japanese. I will never forget my first Japanese breakfast in a celebrated and ancient *ryokan* in Kyoto many years ago: Edward and I sat on the floor of our matted room, and a very formal attendant on her knees served us broiled fish with *tsukemono* (salty Japanese pickles), steamed rice, nori, *tamagoyaki* (rolled omelet), and, of course, miso soup, plus more things than I can remember now, and tea. No doubt as strange to us for breakfast that first time as some of the dishes in this book or some Alsatian specialties might be to some people. Everyone's comfort foods are individualistic, even solipsistic. Still, that Japanese breakfast and setting made a strong and warm impression on me, and I can easily understand the comfort that a full Japanese breakfast can bring.

Nowadays, it is oatmeal and Cream of Wheat (forms of baby food for grown-ups) that I count among my comfort foods.

OATMEAL WITH LEMON ZEST AND PRUNES

• SERVES 2 TO 4 •

1 cup old-fashioned oatmeal

2½ cups water

Pinch of salt

2 tablespoons honey

Zest of 1 lemon

1 teaspoon unsalted butter

¼ cup 2% milk

½ cup pitted prunes, chopped

1. In a medium saucepan, combine the oatmeal, water, and salt and bring to a boil. Cook for 3 to 4 minutes over low heat, stirring occasionally.

2. Add the honey, lemon zest, butter, and milk and mix gently. Cook for another minute and add the prunes, stirring to combine. Serve immediately.

NOTE: *This heats quickly and makes a perfect breakfast-on-the-go during the work week, a nice change from a cold yogurt or toast!*

PEANUT BUTTER BANANA OATMEAL

• SERVES 2 TO 4 •

1 cup old-fashioned oatmeal

2⅓ cups water

Pinch of salt

2 tablespoons peanut butter

1 banana, sliced

⅓ cup 2% or whole milk

½ teaspoon butter

1. Combine the oatmeal, water, and salt in a medium saucepan. Bring to a boil.

2. Cook for 5 minutes, stirring occasionally. Add the peanut butter, banana, milk, and butter and mix gently. Cook for another minute and serve.

STRAWBERRY-BANANA
OATMEAL SMOOTHIE

1 banana, peeled and sliced

2 to 4 frozen strawberries

2 tablespoons Greek-style
  yogurt

½ teaspoon honey

1 teaspoon old-fashioned
  oatmeal

Pinch of cinnamon

1. Place the banana, strawberries, yogurt, honey, and oatmeal in a blender and purée until smooth.

2. Serve in a glass with the cinnamon.

QUINOA WITH ALMONDS, HAZELNUTS, AND APRICOTS

1 cup quinoa

2 tablespoons honey

1 tablespoon lemon juice

1 teaspoon butter

⅓ cup milk

Pinch of salt

1 tablespoon finely chopped
   almonds

1 tablespoon finely chopped
   hazelnuts

¼ cup dried apricots, diced

1. Cook the quinoa according to the package directions.

2. Stir the honey, lemon juice, butter, milk, and salt into the cooked quinoa and cook for another minute. Serve in individual bowls garnished with chopped nuts and apricots.

CREAM OF WHEAT WITH CRANBERRIES AND WALNUTS

• SERVES 4 •

¾ cup Cream of Wheat

3 tablespoons brown sugar

Pinch of cinnamon

2 teaspoons lemon juice

1½ tablespoons unsalted butter

¼ cup dried cranberries

¼ cup walnuts, coarsely chopped

1. In a medium saucepan, cook the Cream of Wheat according to the package directions.

2. When the Cream of Wheat is cooked, stir in the brown sugar, cinnamon, lemon juice, and butter. Mix well and cook for 1 minute.

3. Remove the saucepan from the heat and serve in individual bowls garnished with cranberries and walnuts.

Le Brunch

It does not take a degree in linguistics to recognize the portmanteau nature of brunch, the combination of breakfast and lunch that seemingly connotes a late-morning breakfast or early lunch. Well, today we can forget just the late morning. Walk the streets of Manhattan, for example, on a Sunday morning or early afternoon, and there will be only brunch menus. And certainly restaurants and hotels promote brunch for regular and special occasions such as Mother's Day. Sunday brunch at some hotels is their local signature. Ah, the endless buffets I have seen, with chef stations cooking up omelets and pancakes and even carving slices of beef.

In New York, in good weather we like to entertain outdoors on our terrace for brunch, which often means telling out-of-town guests to come by at 11 AM, which results in their leaving the table at 1 or 2 PM, so the afternoon is free for sightseeing, shopping, or perhaps a Sunday matinee.

What's better than welcoming friends to your home with a glass of Champagne or sparkling water or a little freshly squeezed fruit juice and heading outside for some conversation, nibbles—say a taste of smoked salmon, cheese, or even miniature croissants—before sitting down for an omelet with vegetables and good breads and coffee or tea.

As I am not a late sleeper—at least not since I left my teens—I generally eat an early breakfast before brunch—but then is it lunch? Sure, just with breakfast foods more often than not. I can taste the ricotta pancakes just thinking about them. When Edward and I truly want to combine breakfast and lunch, we'll head off to, say, Balthazar in New York's SoHo for brunch. We'll skip the onion soup gratinée, thank you very much, but if we are in a breakfasty state of mind we will contemplate the brioche French toast. Otherwise, if the raw bar is open, oysters. Now there's a Sunday morning pick-me-up. Plus, there's moules frites (for me) and steak frites (for Edward) to follow and one of our few French fry indulgences, or frunch for us.

Brunch is a global standard today—a development over just the past perhaps fifteen years—and while the venerable *Académie française* shuns the word *brunch* in the French language, preferring *le grand petit déjeuner*, meaning "big breakfast," *les citoyens* just adore it. The French are crazy about the idea of *le brunch*, even if the menu is not all that different from a bistro lunch with a breakfast basket of pastries (known in French as *viennoiseries*, a combination of croissants, *pains aux raisins*, and *pains au chocolat*).

Le French Snack

For those of us who eat three meals a day, snacks are out or are the exception when dinner is very late or travel plans delay mealtime. *Tartines* are—or at least were—the quintessential snack for hungry French teenagers.

But what strikes me as well suited for brunch fare are *tartines*, those small, open-faced, bread-based French finger foods, so I begin the brunch recipes with them.

The key is to buy some really good bread. *Tartines* are served for breakfast, brunch, lunch, or dinner and at tapas bars and one can make a meal out of them. As great bread lovers, the French invented *tartines* and they used to be included at the start of almost every meal.

The last few years, *tartines* have made a huge comeback (perhaps because we are back to lots of great quality bread and artisan bakers) since they are easy, quick, can be changed indefinitely depending on what you have on hand, what is in season, or simply adapting them to your personal tastes. Lots of small cafés or *salons de thé* in Paris and major French cities offer them as a wonderful meal.

When I grew up, a well-buttered *tartine* with a thin bar of dark chocolate was the *goûter* when we came home from school. It's coming back in schools as well, since I noticed most of the young children in my village in Provence had that very snack versus a more fattening *pain au chocolat* or worse, one of those bars from vending machines, which fortunately have now been banned in French schools. So, it seems it's back to basics: simple, nutritious, yummy, and relatively inexpensive. Here's a variety of *tartines* that can be served as a brunch starter (or dinner hors d'oeuvres), as a small assortment on a plate with a simple green salad for lunch, or as a snack any time of day.

GOAT CHEESE AND
HAZELNUT *TARTINES*

• SERVES 4 •

5 ounces fresh goat cheese

4 slices whole grain bread, toasted

⅓ cup toasted and coarsely chopped hazelnuts

1 tablespoon honey

1 teaspoon chopped fresh rosemary

Spread the goat cheese on toasts, sprinkle with hazelnuts, and drizzle the honey. Garnish with rosemary and serve.

RICOTTA AND ANCHOVY *TARTINES*

4 anchovies, rinsed and
   drained

1 tablespoon sherry vinegar

2 tablespoons olive oil

½ cup fresh ricotta, at room
   temperature

Salt and freshly ground
   pepper

4 slices country bread,
   toasted

1. Place the anchovies in a shallow bowl in one layer. Pour the vinegar over the anchovies and marinate for 1 minute. Pour out the vinegar, add 1 tablespoon olive oil to the bowl and set aside.

2. Place the ricotta in a small bowl and season to taste with salt and pepper. Spread the seasoned ricotta on the toasted bread slices. Top each slice with 1 anchovy, drizzle with the remaining 1 tablespoon olive oil, season with additional freshly ground pepper, and serve.

CUCUMBER, PROSCIUTTO, AND PARMESAN *TARTINES*

• SERVES 4 •

. . . .

3 teaspoons unsalted butter,
   softened

2 teaspoons grainy mustard

4 slices fresh bread or
   brioche, lightly toasted

4 slices prosciutto

12 thin slices cucumber

1½ ounces Parmesan

Freshly ground pepper

1. In a small bowl combine the butter and mustard and stir until smooth. Spread a thin layer on each slice of toast. Cover each with 1 slice of prosciutto and 3 slices of cucumber.

2. Using a vegetable peeler, shave thin slices of Parmesan and garnish each *tartine* with 1 or 2 shavings. Season generously with fresh pepper and serve.

SARDINE *TARTINES*

• SERVES 4 •

· ·

1 (3.75-ounce) can
    sardines in water,
    drained

2 tablespoons unsalted
    butter, at room
    temperature

1 teaspoon Dijon mustard

1 tablespoon minced fresh
    parsley

1 tablespoon minced fresh
    chervil

1 teaspoon lemon juice

Salt and freshly ground
    pepper

4 slices country bread,
    toasted

1. Remove the bones from the sardines, place in a bowl, and mash with a fork.

2. In a second bowl, combine the butter, mustard, parsley, chervil, and lemon juice and stir until smooth. Add the mashed sardines and mix gently. Season to taste and serve spread on toasted bread.

PEAR AND BLUE CHEESE
TARTINES

• SERVES 4 •

4 slices sourdough bread, lightly toasted

2 ounces blue cheese, at room temperature

2 pears, rinsed, cored, quartered, and thinly sliced

¼ cup alfalfa sprouts

2 tablespoons coarsely chopped walnuts

Freshly ground pepper

1. Spread each slice of toast with blue cheese and cover with pear slices.

2. Garnish with alfalfa sprouts and walnuts, season with pepper, and serve.

SEA SCALLOP AND
FLEUR DE SEL *TARTINES*

• SERVES 4 •

. . . .

4 sea scallops, each sliced
horizontally into 4 thin
disks

Juice and zest of ½ lemon

4 slices country bread,
lightly toasted

1 tablespoon olive oil (or
walnut oil)

½ teaspoon fleur de sel
(large-grained "flower of
salt" harvested from the
sea works magic)

1. Place the scallops in a small bowl with the lemon juice and marinate for 3 to 5 minutes. Meanwhile, brush the toasted bread slices with the olive oil.

2. Drain the scallops and lay 4 scallop slices, overlapping, on each slice of toast, garnish with the lemon zest and fleur de sel, and serve immediately.

PARMESAN POLENTA WITH PROSCIUTTO

• SERVES 4 •

1 cup polenta

½ cup grated Parmesan

Freshly ground pepper

1 teaspoon olive oil

4 thin slices prosciutto

4 sun-dried tomatoes

12 black olives

1. Cook the polenta according to the package directions. Add the Parmesan and pepper and mix well. Pour into a buttered 8-inch square baking dish and refrigerate for 1 hour.

2. Heat the oil over medium heat in a large nonstick skillet. Cut the chilled polenta into four pieces and cook until heated through and slightly crisp, about 1 minute on each side. Reserve on paper towels.

3. Using the same skillet, briefly cook the prosciutto over medium-high heat, about 1 minute. Garnish each serving of polenta with 1 slice prosciutto, 1 sun-dried tomato, and 3 olives. Serve immediately.

Special and Luxurious
(as in what a luxury to eat)

These recipes are indulgences, and in our home they are reserved for weekends and for entertaining friends, especially at brunch.

MILK JAM (*CONFITURE DE LAIT*)

• MAKES ½ CUP •

1 cup 2% milk

¼ cup plus 1 tablespoon sugar

1. Place the milk and sugar in a small heavy saucepan and bring to a boil, stirring until the sugar is dissolved. Reduce the heat to low and cook very slowly until the mixture has thickened to the consistency of sour cream and is a light caramel color.

2. Remove from the heat and serve as a spread for toast, crêpes, or English muffins. Also delicious drizzled over ice cream!

NOTE: *Milk jam may be stored in a sealed jar and refrigerated for up to 2 weeks.*

CLAFOUTIS PROVENÇAL

We had cherry trees in our garden, and from the time I was eight, I got to climb the ladder (and some branches) and pick cherries. My little girlfriends and I would sometimes overeat the fresh cherries, but there were still enough to bring back to my mom, who used them to make a clafoutis, *baking the fresh fruit in a custardy batter in a round baking dish. The curious name for this dessert comes from the verb* clafir, *"to fill up," because you fill up the batter and mold with fruit, most commonly cherries.* Clafoutis *usually refers to a dessert preparation, but in Provence it can be a savory yet still rich dish with cheese, eggs, and bread.*

2 tablespoons olive oil

1 small eggplant, cut into ½-inch dice

1 yellow pepper, seeded and cut into ½-inch dice

Salt and freshly ground pepper

1 slice bread, crusts removed

2 garlic cloves, peeled

1 cup ricotta

3 eggs

2 tablespoons fresh basil leaves cut into chiffonade (thin strips)

½ cup black olives, pitted and halved

¾ cup grated Parmesan

Butter, softened, for baking dish

Fresh basil (or mint) for garnish

1. Preheat the oven to 350 degrees.

2. Heat the olive oil over medium heat in a skillet and sauté the eggplant and yellow pepper until softened, about 6 minutes. Season to taste and set aside to cool.

3. In a food processor, combine the bread, garlic, ricotta, and eggs and blend until smooth. Season with salt and pepper and, using a spatula, fold in 1 tablespoon basil, the olives, Parmesan, eggplant, and yellow pepper.

4. Pour the mixture into a lightly buttered 8-inch square baking dish and place in the oven. Bake until lightly golden, 30 to 35 minutes. Remove from the oven and let cool. Serve warm or at room temperature, garnished with basil or mint.

GRAPEFRUIT, AVOCADO, AND CAVIAR MILLE-FEUILLE

• SERVES 4 •

2 pink grapefruit

2 ripe avocados, halved and
  pitted

2 tablespoons lemon juice

Pinch of curry powder

Salt and freshly ground
  pepper

4 ounces domestic caviar

1 teaspoon minced fresh
  tarragon

1. Prepare the grapefruit segments: Cut slices off the top and bottom of the grapefruit and slice away the peel and pith, top to bottom, following the curve of the fruit. Working over a bowl and using a small, sharp knife, cut between the membranes to release the segments. Chop into small pieces and reserve.

2. Using a spoon, scoop out the avocado flesh and place in a medium bowl. Add the lemon juice and curry, season to taste, and, using a fork, mash to obtain a smooth texture.

3. Place a 3-inch ring mold in the center of the first plate and build the mille-feuille. Begin with a layer of grapefruit at the bottom of the mold. Cover with a layer of avocado purée and top with a thin layer of caviar, pressing down slightly before carefully lifting away the ring mold. Garnish with tarragon and repeat on the remaining plates. Serve immediately.

SMOKED SALMON, FENNEL, AND ORANGE MILLE-FEUILLE

• SERVES 4 •

3 oranges (blood oranges
    preferred)
1 fennel bulb, trimmed,
    cored, and finely diced
⅓ cup black olives, pitted
    and coarsely chopped
3 teaspoons olive oil
Freshly ground pepper
8 ounces smoked salmon,
    thinly sliced
¼ teaspoon fleur de sel

1. Wash and dry the oranges. Grate the zest from 1 orange and then press the juice, reserving the zest and juice. Segment the remaining 2 oranges, one at a time: Cut slices off the top and bottom of the orange and then slice away the peel and pith, top to bottom, following the curve of the fruit. Working over a bowl and using a small, sharp knife, cut between the membranes to release the segments. Chop each segment into small pieces.

2. In a medium bowl, combine the chopped oranges, orange zest, orange juice, fennel, olives, and olive oil, and season to taste.

3. Using a 3-inch ring mold, cut out 8 smoked salmon circles. To serve, place the ring mold in the center of a salad plate. Place one circle of salmon in the base of the mold and cover with a ½-inch layer of orange-fennel salad, lightly pressing down. Cover with a second layer of smoked salmon and top with ½ inch orange-fennel salad. Lightly press down on the salad and then carefully remove the ring mold. Repeat for the remaining

three plates. Drizzle each with any leftover dressing from the salad and garnish with a sprinkling of fleur de sel. Serve immediately.

NOTE: *Ring molds can be found at most kitchen supply stores and are a great trick for easily creating restaurant-worthy presentations. You may improvise with a clean tuna fish can by removing the top and bottom and using it as a ring mold.*

CHEESE-APPLE MILLE-FEUILLE

• SERVES 4 •

• •

3 ounces each of Jarlsberg, Parmesan, and cheddar

2 teaspoons sherry vinegar

2 tablespoons olive oil

Salt and freshly ground pepper

2 apples (any fruity red variety)

1 tablespoon finely minced fresh parsley

1. Cut each piece of cheese into ¼-inch-thick slices and each slice into matchsticks. Reserve.

2. Place the sherry vinegar into a small bowl and slowly drizzle in the olive oil while whisking. Season to taste.

3. Rinse and core the apples and cut each horizontally into 6 slices (3 per plate).

4. To serve, place 1 apple slice on each dish and cover with the cheese matchsticks. Cover with another apple slice and continue for each plate. Drizzle the dressing on top of and around each mille-feuille, garnish with parsley, and serve.

FROMAGE BLANC WITH BLUE CHEESE AND CHIVES

6 ounces blue cheese
(Fourme d'Ambert or
Roquefort), at room
temperature

14 ounces fromage blanc

4 tablespoons minced fresh
chives plus 1-inch chive
bâtons for garnish, if
desired

16 to 20 slices cocktail rye
bread, toasted

1. Place the softened blue cheese in a small bowl and mash with a fork.

2. Add the *fromage blanc* and stir until smooth. Add the chives and mix until blended.

3. To serve, spread on rye bread toasts and garnish with chive bâtons, if desired.

LEMON TOASTS

• SERVES 4 •

· ·

1 egg white

6 tablespoons sugar

*½ cup plus 2 tablespoons
ground almonds*

Juice and zest of 1 lemon

½ teaspoon orange zest

4 slices brioche

1. Preheat the oven to 375 degrees.

2. In a bowl or stand mixer, whisk together the egg white and sugar until creamy. Add the ground almonds, lemon juice and zest, orange zest, and mix until smooth.

3. Place the brioche slices on a parchment-lined baking sheet and cover the top of each with an even layer of the lemon-almond mixture. Place in the oven and bake until lightly golden, 8 to 10 minutes. Serve warm.

SAVORY *FLAMMEKUECHE*

• SERVES 6 TO 8 •

It's said that pizza is the most popular food in the world. Every culture has its variation of flat bread with a local topping. In Alsace, flammekueche *is a famous specialty and pizza variation, a thin dough crust most commonly topped with bacon, onions, and crème fraîche.*

1 egg

1 tablespoon flour

2 cups fromage blanc *(use cottage cheese as a substitute)*

Salt and freshly ground pepper

Pinch of freshly grated nutmeg

1 pound puff pastry or pizza dough (store-bought), defrosted if frozen

4 large shallots, peeled and thinly sliced (1 to 1½ cups)

¼ pound bacon, cut into ½-inch pieces

1. Preheat the oven to 400 degrees.

2. In a medium bowl, combine the egg, flour, and *fromage blanc*. Stir until smooth and season with salt, pepper, and nutmeg. Set aside.

3. On a floured surface, roll the dough out to fit an 11- x 17-inch baking sheet. Carefully transfer the dough to the baking sheet by rolling the dough around a rolling pin and unrolling it directly onto the pan.

4. Spread an even layer of the *fromage blanc* mixture over the surface of the dough and cover with the shallots and bacon. Fold the edges over, creating a ½-inch border around the tart, and seal by pressing lightly with the tines of a fork. Bake for 30 to 35 minutes or until golden brown. Remove from the oven, let stand for 2 to 3 minutes, cut into squares, and serve.

SWEET *FLAMMEKUECHE*

• SERVES 8 TO 10 •

1 egg

1 cup fromage blanc

⅔ cup crème fraîche

1 teaspoon pure vanilla
    extract

1 pound store-bought puff
    pastry, defrosted
    according to package
    directions

4 apples, peeled, cored,
    quartered, and thinly
    sliced

4 tablespoons sugar

1 tablespoon Calvados or
    eau de vie (optional)

1. Preheat the oven to 400 degrees.

2. In a medium bowl, combine the egg, *fromage blanc,* crème fraîche, and vanilla. Stir until smooth and set aside.

3. On a floured surface, roll the dough out to fit an 11- x 17-inch baking sheet. Carefully transfer the dough to the baking sheet by rolling the dough around a rolling pin and unrolling it directly onto the pan.

4. Spread an even layer of the *fromage blanc–* crème fraîche mixture over the surface of the dough. Top with overlapping apple slices, arranging them in columns and leaving a ½-inch border all around. Fold the edges over, creating a border around the tart, and seal by pressing lightly with the tines of a fork. Sprinkle 2 tablespoons sugar over the apples and bake in the oven until golden brown, about 30 minutes.

5. While the tart is baking, make a simple syrup, if desired: in a small saucepan, combine the remaining 2 tablespoons sugar with 2 tablespoons water and place over medium heat. Bring to a boil and simmer until the sugar is dissolved, 2 to 3 minutes.

Remove from the heat and carefully pour the Calvados, if using, down the side of the saucepan into the syrup; be careful, as the syrup will start to bubble. Stir and allow to cool. After removing the *flammekueche* from the oven, delicately brush the apples with the syrup using a pastry brush. Cut into large squares and serve warm or at room temperature.

CROQUE MONSIEUR
ERIC RIPERT STYLE

4 slices brioche, crusts removed

2 ounces Jarlsberg, cut into 6 slices

1 ounce domestic caviar

2 slices smoked salmon

2 tablespoons unsalted butter

1. Place 2 brioche slices on a work surface and top each with 3 slices of cheese in a single layer. Spread ½ ounce caviar on top of the cheese and cover with a slice of salmon, trimmed to fit the size of the brioche. Top each with a second slice of brioche.

2. Melt 1 tablespoon butter in a nonstick skillet over medium heat and place the sandwiches in the pan. Cook, pressing down lightly with a spatula, until golden brown, about 3 minutes. Add the remaining tablespoon of butter to the pan and flip the sandwiches, cooking until golden and the cheese has melted, about 2 minutes.

3. Transfer the sandwiches to a cutting board, slice diagonally, and serve immediately.

FRENCH TOAST EDWARD STYLE

· SERVES 4 ·

4 slices brioche or challah
(preferably day-old), cut
1 inch thick

4 teaspoons plus 2
tablespoons 2% milk

3 eggs

1 egg white

¼ teaspoon cinnamon

Pinch of freshly grated
nutmeg

1 teaspoon pure vanilla
extract

4 tablespoons (½ stick)
unsalted butter

Maple syrup for serving

1. Place the brioche slices in a large, deep, rectangular pan and pour 1 teaspoon of milk on each slice. (This provides moisture at the bread's center.)

2. In a bowl, whisk together the eggs, egg white, 2 tablespoons milk, cinnamon, nutmeg, and vanilla. Pour over the brioche, turning to coat thoroughly (this step is important so that you end up with a custardy version and not dry French toast), and let stand for about 5 minutes.

3. Heat the butter over medium heat in a large nonstick skillet and cook the brioche for 2 to 3 minutes per side, first on medium high and then on medium-low until golden brown. Cut each slice diagonally (a trick for giving the illusion of a larger portion) and place on a plate slightly superimposing one on top of the other. Serve with pure maple syrup.

NOTE: *You may also serve French toast garnished with a few grains of fleur de sel and a teaspoon of mascarpone on the side accompanied by fresh berries.*

Chapter Two

SOMETIMES IT IS CALLED LUNCH

How are you dealing with ambiguity? Do you ever have cereal for dinner? A snack? Do you ever use recipes for lunch? Cook for lunch? What's a main course versus a side dish? Can sides be lunch or a side dish a main course? In America, many workers buy lunch near their offices or bring a prepared meal to work. Or they eat a somewhat more diversified and usually hot meal at a company or school cafeteria, or a fuller meal when entertaining or being entertained for lunch at a restaurant. For me, the best way to appreciate what we have agreed to call lunch—though that might no longer be the best term—is to consider it the third meal of the day, the meal that supplements and balances breakfast and the larger main meal of the day. So, lunch is really a question of volume and in most cases timing, as it is eaten at midday.

And while there are some classic lunch foods—take sandwiches for an example—almost any dish taken in moderation can be eaten at lunch. Jack up the portion size and suddenly lunch becomes a form of dinner, and the evening meal the smaller meal that balances out the day.

Cereal for dinner? I have a friend in New York who indeed often eats cereal for "dinner," but that's because she eats a big lunch. Healthy and *bien dans sa peau*, Linda is an executive who lives alone, works hard and often late. Every day she has a good, balanced breakfast with protein, fat, and carbohydrates (such as an egg with a piece of buttered toast or yogurt and a slice of toast and always some fresh fruit and coffee) and then regularly has a late business lunch, which she treats as her main meal, including a glass of wine, a few bites of dessert, and no rushing. She works at a large corporation with a staff cafeteria, so when she doesn't go out to lunch, she eats a full, varied meal there. She simply chooses to have her main meal in the early afternoon. After she gets home, at around eight, she is apt to opt for a choice of cereal with perhaps half of a banana or a few blueberries, or sometimes yogurt with a piece of fruit. And she's been known to treat herself to a small piece of dark chocolate (notice the balance in each meal). She enjoys cooking, and it is one of her preferred weekend pastimes. Then she has her main meal in the evening and entertains with passion. Her nutritional and caloric intake per day is balanced. Her two-to-three-day nutritional and caloric intake is regular and healthy. She doesn't worry if she is eating breakfast for dinner or dinner for lunch.

We live in a world that often seems fixated on reducing elements of our lives, singularly and collectively, to ten-second sound bites, to single-word or single-phrase definitions and explanations. It is an ugly sign of superficial times, I fear. What is the reason most French women don't get fat? Easy, I have been told again and again in two words: portion control. (I have also been told many times it is because they smoke so much, but that is nonsense and not supported by any facts.) There is some sound truth, of course, in portion control, but hardly the entire answer.

If you cut your caloric intake in half for each meal, each day for the next three months, you will lose weight regardless of your starting point. You might not enjoy eating as much; you might even develop some health and nutritional deficiencies, and you probably won't find it a sustainable lifestyle, so before year-end you will gain back the weight in yo-yo fashion like so many people who diet instead of adopting a new and informed healthy lifestyle. For me, eating for pleasure is a sustainable approach to learning and maintaining balance (*équilibre*) when it comes to food, and physical routine is another all-important component, at least the equal of portion size.

French women (and men) do eat smaller portions than Americans and many others. A portion of steak might be 4 or 6 ounces, not 8, 10, 12, or more that is common in America. A dish of pasta, as in Italy, is more likely to be a first course than a main course of a meal and to be the portion size of a fist instead of two hands full. And portions especially extend to sugar intake. Dessert portions are not only smaller and more likely to be simply fruit than in America, but the amount of sugar in the recipes for the same type of pies or cakes is significantly less. My recipes reflect a French woman's attitude toward portion proportions.

I want to reemphasize that it is okay to eat more than your body needs as fuel if there is pleasure involved or if a social occasion such as a family holiday or business meal leads to eating a large meal. Balance, however, is what must be remembered and followed. Square your intake over a day or two and be sure to balance your books by the end of the week. Big lunch, then small dinner, and vice versa. Sweet dessert on Monday, perhaps none on Tuesday.

I begin this section on recipes for lunch with soup, the perfect meal by itself: it hydrates well, is more filling than many salads, and is infused with good vitamins, minerals, and other nutrients without piling on the calories. When I know I have a lavish dinner planned, I'll eat a bowl of soup alone for lunch, and feel perfectly satisfied up until dinnertime. However, for a more substantive midday meal, I'll have a cup of soup as an appetizer, and then a main course of fish, chicken, or pasta afterward. Then, of course, I'll strike a balance that evening, enjoying smaller portions or fewer courses for my evening meal. One more observation on soups. When you make them from scratch, you know what's in them, and since they can also be reheated, one preparation can feature more than one appearance in your eating plan over a few days. Beware of the canned or packaged kinds of soups that are often laced with very high doses of sodium, which tend to boost your blood pressure in the afternoon and make you very thirsty—and hungry, just what you don't want at work or play.

A lot of the dishes and recipes that follow can be taken to work the next day or days and reheated or "accessorized" into a different food experience. We live in a world of ubiquitous microwave ovens. One of their advantages is that you can bring vegetables to work uncooked and zap them for a short while and you have a simply cooked vegetable with a very high percentage of its nutrients locked in. Why not a plate of vegetables, typically a side dish, as a meal? As I age, I increasingly order two appetizers instead of an appetizer and a main course. I need less food than some restaurants proffer with their main courses. And why can't a portion of any side dish be the big plate of the day?

And a reminder about portions. The greatest and deepest pleasure in food exists in the first three bites. So, eat with all your senses and then let your brain kick in after three bites. Remember it is your brain not your stomach that controls your hunger once you've sat down for a meal. Do you want or need the next bite? And the next bite?

Soups

ENDIVE AND AVOCADO GAZPACHO

• SERVES 4 •

3 endives, rinsed and sliced

2 avocados, peeled and chopped

½ cup capers, rinsed and drained

6 tablespoons olive oil

Juice of 2 limes

¼ to ½ cup chicken stock

½ teaspoon curry powder

Salt and freshly ground pepper

Croûtons (optional)

Fresh mint (optional)

1. Place the endives, avocados, capers, olive oil, and lime juice in a food processer and blend until smooth, adding enough chicken stock to obtain the desired consistency. Stir in the curry and season to taste.

2. Transfer the mixture to a bowl, cover tightly, and refrigerate for at least 2 hours. Serve chilled, garnished with a few croûtons rubbed with fresh mint, if desired.

BEET AND GINGER GAZPACHO

• SERVES 4 TO 6 •

10 ounces cooked beets,
  peeled and diced

1 tomato, peeled and
  chopped

1 garlic clove, peeled and
  chopped

1 large onion, peeled and
  chopped

1 tablespoon peeled and
  grated fresh ginger

1 teaspoon wasabi (or 2
  teaspoons horseradish)

1 tablespoon red wine
  vinegar

2 tablespoons olive oil

2 cups chicken broth

1 tablespoon crème fraîche

Salt and freshly ground
  pepper

1. Place the beets, tomato, garlic, onion, ginger, wasabi, vinegar, olive oil, chicken broth, and crème fraîche in a food processor and purée until smooth.

2. Pass half of the puréed soup through a sieve and combine with the remainder of the soup, season to taste, and chill. Serve cold, garnished with a dollop of crème fraîche, if desired.

BEET AND ZUCCHINI GAZPACHO

• SERVES 4 TO 6 •

1 tablespoon olive oil

2 onions, peeled and finely
chopped

2 medium zucchini, rinsed
and sliced

1 celery stalk, rinsed and
sliced

4 tablespoons peeled and
minced shallots

1 teaspoon ground
cardamom

1 medium beet, cooked,
peeled, and sliced

Juice of 1 lemon

Salt and freshly ground
pepper

2 hard-boiled eggs, peeled,
whites and yolks
separated, and finely
chopped

4 tablespoons chopped fresh
parsley

1. Heat the olive oil in a large pot over medium heat. Add 1 chopped onion, the zucchini, celery, and shallots and sauté for 5 minutes.

2. Add the cardamom and 4 cups water and bring to a boil. Simmer for 20 minutes. Remove from the heat and refrigerate until chilled.

3. To serve, add the beet and lemon juice to the chilled soup and season to taste. Pour the soup into individual bowls and garnish with the chopped eggs, the remaining onion, and the parsley.

MAGICAL LEEK BROTH

· SERVES 1 FOR THE WEEKEND ·

This is one of the best-known recipes from my French Women Don't Get Fat, so I am reprinting it. When that book came out it got lots of press about leeks and I got a lot of emails from readers. I was even cited as the cause of a leek shortage in America. (I am not making this up.) It seems I helped many to discover or rediscover leeks and many professed to love them, while some found leeks dreadful. I admit you have to get used to their odor when they are being cooked, but it is such a sweet vegetable, enjoyed hot or cold, I am surprised when people don't like it. It certainly is good for you and remains one of my favorites. The magical leek broth was/is often misunderstood. It is a fine and light soup for lunch for sure, especially with some of the leek stalk as a side salad with just a drizzle of olive oil.

I included the broth in that book, however, to kick off a resetting of one's weight and equilibrium, and as a trick French women have traditionally employed, at least in my world. I recommended it for a weekend. First, since it is a mild diuretic, the leek broth helps to flush the blood and kidneys, thus purging the body of various toxins, a so-called mild detox—something I believe in doing every now and again. And since drinking only broth for 48 hours means a sharp decrease in food intake, people tend to lose a pound or two from that exercise and perhaps another pound from water loss. So, voilà, Monday morning you are two or three pounds lighter. That's a great psychological booster shot toward losing some weight and resetting a desirable body balance. But that was it. It wasn't something designed for a week at a time or every month. (If one vitamin pill is good for you, imagine how good taking ten of them must be!) Just once in a while enjoy a leek broth weekend (or even just for 24 hours) when you feel you need to detox and lose a few pounds quickly toward finding your equilibrium. I am happy that leeks (and not just Magical Leek Broth) have become some people's "new best friend," and it is a pleasure to fill requests for more leek recipes in this book, whether as a salad or with fish, pasta, or simply as a veggie.

2 pounds leeks

Water to cover in a large pot

1. Clean the leeks and rinse well to get rid of any sand and soil. Cut the ends of the green parts, leaving all the white parts plus a suggestion of green. (Reserve the extra greens for soup stock.)

2. Put the leeks in a large pot and cover with water. Bring to a boil and simmer without a lid for 20 to 30 minutes. Pour off the liquid and reserve. Place the leeks in a bowl.

NOTE: *The juice is to be drunk (reheated or at room temperature to taste) every 2 to 3 hours, a cup at a time. For meals or whenever hungry, have some of the leeks themselves, ½ cup at a time. Drizzle with a few drops of extra virgin olive oil and lemon juice. Season sparingly with salt and pepper. Add chopped parsley if you wish. This will be your nourishment for both days, until Sunday dinner, when you can have a small piece of meat or fish (4 to 6 ounces; don't lose that scale yet!), with two vegetables steamed with a drizzle of oil and some herbs, and a piece of fruit.*

CARROT SOUP
WITH YOGURT AND KIWI

2 tablespoons olive oil

1 onion, peeled and chopped

2 pounds carrots, peeled and
  chopped, plus 1 carrot,
  peeled and cut into small
  dice, for garnish

2 celery stalks, rinsed and
  chopped

2 tablespoons chopped fresh
  cilantro

¾ cup nonfat plain Greek-
  style yogurt

Salt and freshly ground
  pepper

4 ounces boiled ham, cut
  into matchsticks

2 kiwi, peeled and diced

1. Heat the olive oil in a large pot over medium heat and add the onion, carrots, and celery. Sauté the vegetables for 5 minutes; add the cilantro and 4 cups of water and bring to a boil. Cover and simmer until the vegetables are tender, about 20 minutes.

2. Carefully transfer the vegetables to a blender or food processer. Purée, adding some of the cooking liquid until the desired consistency is reached. Transfer to a bowl and allow to cool. When cool, stir in the yogurt and season to taste. Cover and place in the refrigerator to chill.

3. Just before serving, cook the ham in a nonstick sauté pan over medium-high heat until hot, 1 to 2 minutes. Place the chilled soup in individual bowls and add the ham and kiwi, garnish with the diced carrot, and serve.

ENDIVE WITH GREEN TOMATO JAM

• SERVES 4 •

2 tablespoons green tomato jam

2 tablespoons lemon juice

2 tablespoons olive oil

Fleur de sel and freshly ground pepper

4 medium endives, rinsed, trimmed, and cut lengthwise into strips

16 black olives, pitted

¼ cup fresh basil leaves cut into chiffonade (thin strips)

4 baguette slices, toasted and rubbed with mustard

1. In a small bowl, combine the green tomato jam and lemon juice. Whisk in the olive oil and season to taste.

2. Place the endives in a salad bowl and add the dressing, tossing well to combine. Garnish with the olives and basil and serve with toasted baguette slices.

NOTE: *Green tomato jam can be difficult to find. Red pepper jelly is a delicious sweet-tart alternative that goes nicely with the pleasantly bitter flavor of endive.*

MÂCHE, CELERIAC,
AND BEET SALAD

1 teaspoon mustard
  (preferably Dijon)

2 tablespoons sherry vinegar

5 tablespoons olive oil

Salt and freshly ground
  pepper

4 cups mâche

1 medium (about 1 pound)
  celeriac, peeled and
  grated

1 pound red and yellow
  beets, cooked, peeled,
  and quartered

1. Combine the mustard and vinegar in a small bowl. Whisk in the olive oil and season to taste.

2. In a large bowl, combine the mâche and celeriac, toss with the dressing, and divide the mixture equally among four plates. Place 3 to 4 beet wedges on each plate and serve.

CARROT AND CELERIAC SALAD

• SERVES 4 •

4 medium carrots, peeled and cut into matchsticks

1 medium celeriac (about 1 pound), peeled and cut into matchsticks

1 tablespoon whole grain mustard

2 tablespoons red wine vinegar

6 tablespoons olive oil

Salt and freshly ground pepper

⅓ cup walnuts, chopped

2 tablespoons minced fresh parsley

1. Bring a pot of salted water to a boil. Add the carrots and celeriac and blanch for 3 to 4 minutes until crisp-tender. Drain and place the vegetables in a salad bowl.

2. Meanwhile, in a small bowl, whisk together the mustard, vinegar, and olive oil until smooth. Season to taste. Pour the vinaigrette over the warm carrots and celeriac and toss gently to combine. Garnish with the chopped walnuts and parsley and serve.

SHAVED FENNEL
AND CITRUS SALAD

• SERVES 4 •

2 grapefruits

2 oranges

2 fennel bulbs, trimmed and
rinsed

2 tablespoons sherry vinegar

6 tablespoons olive oil

1 tablespoon finely minced
shallot

½ teaspoon honey

Salt and freshly ground
pepper

½ pound frisée, torn into
bite-size pieces (about 4
cups)

2 tablespoons finely chopped
fresh parsley

1 teaspoon finely chopped
fresh mint

1. Prepare the citrus segments by cutting off the tops and bottoms of the grapefruits and oranges. Cut the peel and white pith from the oranges and grapefruits and, working over a bowl and using a small sharp knife, cut between the membranes to release the segments. Place the citrus segments in a large bowl.

2. Quarter the fennel bulbs lengthwise, then cut crosswise into paper-thin slices using a mandoline.* Add the shaved fennel to the citrus.

3. In a small bowl, whisk together the vinegar, olive oil, shallots, and honey and season to taste. Pour the dressing over the citrus-fennel mixture and gently toss to mix. Arrange the frisée on a serving platter and top with the citrus-fennel salad. Sprinkle with parsley and mint and serve.

*A mandoline is a great addition to your *batterie de cuisine*. The plastic Japanese version is widely available, relatively inexpensive, and makes it incredibly easy to uniformly slice veggies for salads and gratins.

ITALIAN-STYLE FENNEL
AND APPLE SALAD

• SERVES 4 •

2 fennel bulbs, washed, trimmed, quartered lengthwise, and thinly sliced crosswise

2 red apples, washed, cored, and sliced

2 tablespoons lemon juice (½ lemon)

6 ounces pecorino, cut into matchsticks

3 tablespoons olive oil

Salt and freshly ground pepper

⅓ cup pine nuts, toasted

1. Place the fennel, apples, lemon juice, and pecorino in a serving bowl.

2. Add the olive oil and gently toss. Season to taste, garnish with pine nuts, and serve.

NOTE: *Don't peel the apples; the red skin provides a beautiful and colorful contrast in the salad. If you prefer a more acidic flavor, use Granny Smith apples.*

GRATED FRUIT
AND VEGGIE "SLAW"

• SERVES 4 •

1 lemon

2 tablespoons almond paste
  (not marzipan)

1 cup plain yogurt

Salt and freshly ground
  pepper

2 carrots, peeled and grated

2 Granny Smith apples,
  peeled and grated

½ pound celeriac, peeled
  and grated

½ cup golden raisins

½ cup toasted almonds,
  chopped

1. Rinse the lemon, finely grate the zest, and reserve. Press the juice from the lemon into a small bowl and add the almond paste, whisking until smooth. Add the yogurt, season to taste, and reserve.

2. In a large bowl, combine the grated carrots, apples, and celeriac. Add the yogurt dressing and toss. Sprinkle the salad with raisins, almonds, and lemon zest and serve.

SAUTÉ OF PEAS AND PROSCIUTTO WITH FRESH MINT

1 tablespoon olive oil

½ cup peeled and thinly sliced shallots

1 pound fresh shelled peas or frozen peas, thawed

1 pound snow peas, rinsed and drained

2 tablespoons unsalted butter

2 ounces prosciutto, chopped

Salt and freshly ground pepper

1 tablespoon finely chopped fresh mint

1. Heat the olive oil in a nonstick skillet over medium heat and add the shallots. Sauté until softened, about 3 minutes. Add the peas and snow peas and cook for about 5 minutes, stirring occasionally, until just tender, being careful not to overcook.

2. Add the butter and prosciutto, mixing delicately, and cover and cook for 1 minute. Season to taste, sprinkle with mint, and serve.

HARICOTS VERTS SALAD WITH PEACHES AND ALMONDS

• SERVES 4 •

1 pound haricots verts,
   trimmed

2 peaches (white preferred),
   rinsed, pitted, and thinly
   sliced

¼ cup almonds, coarsely
   chopped

A few fresh mint leaves,
   finely chopped

Fleur de sel

Freshly ground pepper

Juice of 1 lemon

1 tablespoon olive oil

1. Bring a large pot of salted water to a boil. Add the haricots verts and cook until crisp-tender. Drain and allow to cool.

2. In a medium serving bowl, combine the haricots verts, peaches, almonds, mint, fleur de sel, pepper, lemon juice, and olive oil, tossing gently. Refrigerate for 15 minutes and serve.

ASPARAGUS WITH YOGURT DRESSING

• SERVES 4 •

1 pound asparagus, trimmed

½ cup coarsely chopped fresh basil

¾ cup 2% Greek-style yogurt

Salt and freshly ground pepper

2 tablespoons unsalted butter

1 tablespoon hazelnut oil

1. Bring a large pot of salted water to a boil and blanch the asparagus for 1 minute. Drain and reserve 4 spears. Place the remaining asparagus in a bowl of ice water to stop the cooking process. When chilled, drain and pat dry.

2. Finely chop the reserved 4 asparagus spears and place in a medium bowl. Add the basil and yogurt and stir to combine. Season to taste and reserve.

3. Melt the butter in a large skillet over medium heat. Add the blanched asparagus and sauté until lightly browned, about 3 minutes. Season to taste, drizzle with hazelnut oil, and place in a serving dish.

4. Spoon the yogurt dressing over the asparagus and serve immediately.

RATATOUILLE

• SERVES 6 •

. . . .

Although there are variations on the number of ingredients in a ratatouille, I keep mine simple and find the flavor of each vegetable more intense as a result. This classic dish from the South of France gained popularity worldwide after the film Ratatouille *was released, and many people discovered the word and how to pronounce it. It certainly was not a staple or common recipe in most of the world, after all, but the film as well as interest in a healthy Mediterranean diet spiked curiosity. I was asked to do a demo at many cooking schools and on TV programs, and people were stunned how easy it is to make and how versatile it is (and add inexpensive considering how you can "stretch" it). A Brazilian TV crew came to my home to tape me making it to share with their weekly magazine's huge audience. What a world! Here's to the frugality of French women! Remember "the least effort for the most pleasure" is a principle to live by—as long as it is healthy.*

1 pound tomatoes

1 pound zucchini

1 pound eggplant

4 garlic cloves

2 tablespoons minced fresh parsley

Salt and freshly ground pepper

Olive oil (optional)

1. Use an equal amount of tomatoes, zucchini, and eggplant. Wash and cut into thick slices.

2. Using a large heavy metal enameled pot (such as a Le Creuset cast-iron pot), make layers starting with the eggplant, then the tomatoes, and finally the zucchini and repeat until the pot is almost filled to the edge, adding some garlic cloves and parsley between the layers. Season with salt and pepper. (If you only have a light stainless-steel pot that is not nonstick, brush a drizzle of olive oil at the bottom of the pot so that the first layer of eggplant will not stick.)

3. Cover and cook over very low heat until the vegetables are tender, 1 to 2½ hours.

4. Let it sit for 20 minutes, then serve. Use soup bowls, since at that stage it is more of a soup; the liquid is mostly water from the veggies.

CRIMINI SALAD

• SERVES 4 •

1 pound crimini mushrooms,
wiped clean with a damp
paper towel and sliced

2 tablespoons sherry vinegar

1 tablespoon lemon juice

4 tablespoons walnut oil

Salt and freshly ground
pepper

2 tablespoons chopped
walnuts

2 tablespoons chopped fresh
parsley

2 tablespoons finely chopped
fresh chives

¼ cup Parmesan shavings

1. Place the mushrooms in a large salad bowl and set aside.

2. In a small bowl, whisk together the sherry vinegar, lemon juice, and walnut oil. Season to taste and add to the mushrooms, tossing to combine.

3. Garnish the salad with the walnuts, parsley, chives, and Parmesan and serve.

Pasta

People don't normally think of pasta as French cuisine, but it is increasingly being served in France: globalization, the economy, and the high cost of food, especially meat, has something to do with that. When I grew up, most families in my town would stick to spaghetti and tomato sauce, and it was usually a dish served at month's end when the food budget was getting short. Occasionally, pasta was used in soups, mostly bouillon or consommé types, and was angel hair, vermicelli, or the fun "alphabet" pastina we used to play with, making those soup dinners endless to our *nounou*'s displeasure. The French also like pasta in gratin dishes, and for that one needs hollow types such as penne or macaroni, which are able to absorb the heavy sauces. In my mother's native Alsace, tagliatelle (also called fettuccine) is often served with fish and cream sauces. Of course, ravioli and lasagna have always been favorites especially when eating out in restaurants. The newest trend in France is for room temperature salads with light noodles such as farfalle or fusilli, something that has been around for a while in America at ubiquitous salad bars.

Because pasta dishes can be eaten at room temperature, added to a salad, or reheated in our take-out, microwave world, they have become a good and nutritious lunchtime meal at work or at home. Some of the "lunch" pastas that follow can certainly figure as "dinner" pasta—again it is a question of portion size and balance. If they are made for dinner, the leftover in some variation (say, add some tuna or vegetables) can become another lunch the next day or so.

PENNE WITH EGGPLANT AND TUNA

• SERVES 4 •

1 medium eggplant, rinsed
   and cut into ½-inch dice

Salt

5 ounces fresh tuna, cut into
   1-inch dice

Freshly ground pepper

1½ tablespoons olive oil plus
   additional for serving

12 ounces penne

⅓ cup tomato sauce

2 tablespoons capers, rinsed
   in water and drained

¼ cup fresh basil leaves cut
   into chiffonade (thin
   strips)

1. Place the eggplant in a colander and toss with 1 teaspoon salt. Place the colander over a bowl and allow to drain for 30 minutes. Pat the eggplant dry.

2. Season the tuna with salt and pepper. In a large nonstick skillet, warm up ½ tablespoon olive oil over medium-high heat and quickly sear the tuna, about 10 seconds per side. Remove from the pan and set aside.

3. In a large pot of boiling salted water, cook the penne until al dente, 10 to 12 minutes. Drain.

4. While the pasta is cooking, heat the remaining 1 tablespoon olive oil in the pan over medium-high heat and add the eggplant, sautéing until golden, about 8 minutes. Stir in the tomato sauce, capers, and pasta, tossing to combine. Add the tuna and season to taste. Serve immediately garnished with basil and a drizzle of olive oil.

TAGLIATELLE WITH LEEKS AND PROSCIUTTO

• SERVES 4 •

. . . .

1½ pounds leeks, white
    parts only

10 ounces tagliatelle

8 slices prosciutto, cut into
    ½-inch-wide strips

4 to 6 tablespoons olive oil

½ cup freshly grated
    pecorino

¾ cup freshly grated
    Parmesan

¼ cup fresh basil leaves cut
    into chiffonade (thin
    strips)

Salt and freshly ground
    pepper

1. Cut the leeks into ½-inch-wide strips, rinse to remove any grit, and steam until softened, about 8 to 10 minutes.

2. Meanwhile, cook the tagliatelle in a large pot of salted boiling water until al dente, 8 to 10 minutes.

3. Drain the pasta and place in a serving bowl. Add the leeks, prosciutto, and olive oil and mix well. Sprinkle with the cheeses and basil, season to taste, and serve immediately.

LINGUINE WITH SHRIMP, TOMATOES, AND BASIL

• SERVES 4 •

12 ounces linguine

2 tablespoons butter

2 tablespoons olive oil

3 garlic cloves, peeled and minced

Pinch of red pepper flakes

1 pound large raw shrimp, peeled and deveined with tails intact

½ cup dry white wine

1 (14.5-ounce can) diced tomatoes

½ cup fresh basil leaves cut into chiffonade (thin strips)

Salt and freshly ground pepper

1. Bring a large pot of salted water to a boil over high heat. Add the linguine and cook until al dente, 10 to 12 minutes.

2. Meanwhile, melt the butter and olive oil in a large sauté pan over medium-high heat. Add the garlic and red pepper flakes and sauté until fragrant, about 1 minute.

3. Add the shrimp to the pan and sauté until they start to turn pink and are almost cooked, 2 to 3 minutes. Deglaze the pan with white wine and simmer for 1 minute. Add the tomatoes and juice and simmer for 4 to 6 minutes until slightly thickened.

4. Drain the pasta and add to the pan with the basil. Toss to combine and season to taste. Serve immediately.

FUSILLI WITH SPINACH AND ANCHOVIES

• SERVES 4 •

12 ounces fusilli

¼ cup olive oil

2 tablespoons pine nuts

2 garlic cloves, peeled and minced

¾ pound spinach, rinsed and drained

6 anchovies, rinsed and finely chopped

2 teaspoons lemon juice

Salt and freshly ground pepper

1 tablespoon butter

⅓ cup freshly grated Parmesan

1. Bring a large pot of slightly salted water to a boil. Add the fusilli and cook for 8 to 10 minutes.

2. Meanwhile, heat the olive oil in a large skillet over medium-high heat. Add the pine nuts and cook until golden, about 2 minutes. Remove from the skillet and reserve.

3. Reduce the heat to medium-low and add the garlic to the skillet. Sauté until fragrant, about 1 minute, add the spinach and anchovies, cover, and cook over medium heat until the spinach is just cooked and slightly wilted. Add the lemon juice and season to taste.

4. When the pasta is cooked, drain and place in a large serving dish. Add the butter and the spinach-anchovy mixture and toss to combine. Sprinkle with the pine nuts and Parmesan and serve immediately.

SPAGHETTI *AL LIMONE*

• SERVES 4 •

12 ounces spaghetti

3 tablespoons olive oil

2 medium onions, peeled and minced

½ cup dry white wine

Zest and juice of 1 lemon

Salt and freshly ground pepper

1 cup watercress, chopped

½ cup freshly grated Parmesan

1. Bring a large pot of salted water to a boil over high heat. Add the spaghetti and cook until al dente, about 8 minutes.

2. Meanwhile, heat 1 tablespoon olive oil in a skillet over medium heat and add the onions. Cook until softened, about 4 minutes. Add the wine, lemon zest, and lemon juice and season to taste. Increase the heat to medium-high and bring to a boil for 1 minute. Reduce the heat to medium and simmer for 5 minutes.

3. Drain the pasta and add to the skillet along with the remaining 2 tablespoons olive oil and watercress, tossing to combine. Season to taste and divide among four plates. Serve immediately, garnished with the fresh Parmesan.

SPAGHETTI WITH LIME
AND ARUGULA

• SERVES 4 •

3 limes

12 ounces spaghetti

2 tablespoons olive oil plus
   additional for pasta

1 garlic clove, peeled and
   minced

¼ teaspoon red pepper flakes

¼ cup sun-dried tomatoes,
   chopped

1 teaspoon capers, rinsed
   and drained

6 ounces fresh arugula,
   rinsed, patted dry, and
   roughly chopped

Salt and freshly ground
   pepper

¼ cup grated Parmesan

1. Grate the zest of 2 limes and press the juice of 1 of them. Cut the third lime into quarters. Reserve.

2. Bring a large pot of salted water to a boil. Add the spaghetti and cook until just al dente (you want it to be slightly undercooked). Drain, return to the pot, and toss with a drizzle of olive oil. Reserve.

3. In a large skillet, heat 2 tablespoons olive oil over medium heat and sauté the lime zest for 30 seconds. Add the garlic, red pepper flakes, sun-dried tomatoes, and capers and sauté for 1 to 2 minutes. Add the pasta and cook for 2 to 3 minutes, stirring gently. Add the lime juice and arugula, season to taste, and serve immediately with quarters of lime, a drizzle of olive oil, and grated Parmesan.

FARFALLE WITH YOGURT-BASIL SAUCE

12 ounces farfalle

1 tablespoon olive oil

½ cup pearl onions, peeled
and thinly sliced

2 garlic cloves, peeled and
minced

Zest and juice of 1 lemon

1 cup plain Greek-style
yogurt

¼ cup fresh basil leaves cut
into chiffonade (thin
strips)

¼ cup chopped fresh parsley

Salt and freshly ground
pepper

1. Bring a pot of salted water to a boil over high heat. Add the farfalle and cook until al dente, about 10 minutes.

2. Meanwhile, heat the olive oil in a large skillet over medium heat and sauté the onions and garlic until fragrant and soft, 3 to 4 minutes. Deglaze with the lemon juice and cook until the liquid has completely reduced, about 2 minutes. Remove the skillet from the heat and stir in the yogurt, lemon zest, basil, and parsley. Season to taste, add the drained farfalle to the skillet, and toss to combine. Serve immediately.

From the Sea

Question: If you were at a company cafeteria or if you were taken out to lunch at a restaurant and a fish dish that you like was available, would you order it? Award yourself a health star if you said yes. We all know fish is good for us, and now that we've established that you would eat fish for lunch, let's consider making some for yourself and perhaps anyone eating with you. Okay, granted, a hot fish dish is not the ideal meal to fix or eat at your desk, but plenty of people still order Chinese take-out fish dishes for lunch. I am including fish dishes in my lunch recommendations to encourage people to appreciate that they can be extremely easy to prepare. And a little cooking is enjoyable, even relaxing. Throwing a few sardines or a mackerel or two in a nonstick frying pan for three minutes isn't exactly hard work or haute cuisine, and the result is as healthy and tasty as can be (count squeezing a lemon over them as daily exercise). Why not include them as part of one's regular lunch mix? Hopefully, we all have some days off—holidays, personal days, even birthdays at some companies—and there are weekends, and some people work from home now and again or always. Cooking need not be thought of as a chore but a pleasure. So, ban the excuses and *mange ton poisson.*

On one day of the weekend especially, I like to have a little bit of fish for lunch. If you eat a sandwich for a midday meal on a Saturday, say, then a main meal for dinner, substituting a small portion of fish for the sandwich is a plus. And, again, mix and match. These fish recipes with modest proportions are ideal for lunch and in a bit larger portion work well as a main course at dinner. Because in formal French meals, there is traditionally both a fish and meat course, perhaps I am accustomed to small portions of fish at a meal; so for my purposes now, let's call them lunch-size portions. And try any leftovers cold the next day. Are there lunch fish and dinner fish? There are no rules, perhaps just portion sizes and what appeals to you, but generally I think of larger fish served in steak-like cuts, such as swordfish or tuna, as dinner fish and "softer" and more delicate fish as appropriate for midday. And that is represented a bit in where I chose to place the fish recipes in this book. I also tend to think of fish dishes that take relatively modest preparation or cooking time as lunch friendly. However, how do you know a poem is good or great? You can analyze it again and again in greater depth to support your conclusion, but pretty much you just know a good poem when you read one. I can look at a fish and fish dish and know whether I personally would like it for lunch or dinner. Try it. *De gustibus non est disputandum.*

STEAMED MONKFISH
WITH VEGETABLES

• SERVES 4 •

1 cup fresh cilantro, washed

⅓ cup blanched almonds

Salt and freshly ground
pepper

Pinch of cayenne pepper

4 (5- to 6-ounce) monkfish
fillets, each about 1 inch
thick

1 cucumber, washed and
sliced into "ribbons"
using a vegetable peeler
or mandoline

2 carrots, peeled and cut
into matchsticks

2 zucchini, washed and cut
into matchsticks

Olive oil for serving

1. Place the cilantro and almonds in a food processor and grind into powder. Season to taste, add the cayenne, and place on a large plate.

2. Lightly press the cilantro-almond mixture on both sides of the monkfish. Wrap each piece with a single layer of cucumber slices and carefully place, seam side down, in a steamer insert over simmering water. Cover and steam for 7 minutes. Add the carrots and zucchini and continue steaming for 3 to 5 minutes.

3. Place 1 fillet on each plate, season to taste, and drizzle with olive oil. Divide the zucchini and carrots among the four plates and serve immediately.

TILAPIA WITH CUMIN
AND MUSHROOMS

1 teaspoon ground cumin

4 (3- to 4-ounce) tilapia
   fillets

Salt and freshly ground
   pepper

1 tablespoon unsalted butter

2 tablespoons olive oil

2 cups button mushrooms,
   wiped cleaned and sliced

2 tablespoons chopped fresh
   parsley plus additional
   for garnish

4 lemon wedges (optional)

1. Sprinkle the cumin on both sides of the tilapia fillets and season with salt and pepper. Reserve.

2. Heat the butter and 1 tablespoon olive oil in a large nonstick skillet over medium-high heat. Add the mushrooms and sauté until softened, about 2 minutes. Season to taste, stir in the parsley, and transfer to a plate and keep warm.

3. Increase the heat to high and add the remaining tablespoon of olive oil to the skillet. When the pan is hot, add the fillets and cook for 2 to 3 minutes on each side.

4. To serve, place a portion of mushrooms on each plate and top with a fillet. Garnish with additional parsley and a lemon wedge, if desired.

SEA BASS WITH
CELERIAC-MINT SALSA

• SERVES 4 •

4 (4- to 5-ounce) sea bass
fillets

Salt and freshly ground
pepper

4 limes, thinly sliced

1 medium unpeeled
zucchini, sliced and
steamed for 2 minutes

½ pound celeriac, peeled
and grated

½ cup fresh mint leaves cut
into chiffonnade (thin
strips)

2 tablespoons capers, rinsed
and drained

Juice of 4 limes

1 tablespoon olive oil

2 leeks, white parts only,
sliced into matchsticks,
and steamed for 8
minutes

1. Preheat the oven to 350 degrees.

2. Place the sea bass fillets on a baking sheet. Season the fillets and cover each with a single layer of lime slices. Top each with a single layer of zucchini and season to taste. Bake for 12 to 15 minutes, depending upon the thickness of the fillets.

3. Meanwhile, prepare the celeriac-mint salsa: in a medium bowl, combine the grated celeriac, mint, and capers. Add the lime juice and olive oil, stirring until well mixed. Season to taste and set aside. (This may be made a few hours in advance, covered, and refrigerated.)

4. To serve, place the leeks in the center of each plate. Top with 1 fillet and spoon the salsa over and around.

BOUILLABAISSE
TWENTY-FIRST CENTURY

Why twenty-first century? It has no potatoes and much less bread and olive oil than the legions of Marseilles women used in making their specialty for their families in the last century. And since we all don't live near the docks in Marseilles, the fish selection is modified as well.

1 pound mixed fish fillets (whiting, cod, halibut, tilapia, or snapper), cut into 1-inch pieces

½ pound shellfish (clams, mussels, or shrimp in shells)

2 tablespoons Pernod

2 tablespoons olive oil

2 garlic cloves, peeled and minced

2 small onions, peeled and sliced

1 fennel bulb, washed and sliced

Zest of 1 orange

1 (14.5-ounce) can tomatoes

6 cups fish stock

Salt and freshly ground pepper

½ cup chopped fresh parsley

4 thick slices country bread, lightly toasted

1. Place the fish and shrimp, if using, in a large bowl and add the Pernod and 1 tablespoon olive oil, mixing gently to combine. If using clams or mussels, scrub and remove the beards from the mussels.

2. Heat the remaining tablespoon olive oil in a large, deep saucepan over medium heat. Add the garlic, onions, and fennel and sauté until fragrant and softened, 5 to 6 minutes. Add the orange zest, tomatoes and any juice, and the fish stock. Bring to a boil and cook until the vegetables are soft and the liquid has reduced by half, 20 to 25 minutes.

3. Add the fish and cook for 2 to 3 minutes. Add the shellfish and cook until the shells open or the shrimp just turn pink. Correct seasoning. Divide among four bowls, garnish each with parsley, and serve with toasted bread spread with the rouille.

ROUILLE

2 red peppers, roasted and
   peeled
2 garlic cloves, peeled
1 teaspoon lemon juice
Pinch of paprika
Salt and freshly ground
   pepper

ROUILLE

1. Place all the ingredients in a blender and purée until smooth.

2. Season to taste and serve on toast with the bouillabaisse.

FLOUNDER FILLETS
WITH FENNEL

1 large fennel bulb

1 onion, peeled and diced

2 tablespoons minced
   shallots

Pinch of ground cardamom

4 (4- to 5-ounce) flounder
   fillets

1 tablespoon tapenade

½ cup dry vermouth (or
   white wine)

1 tablespoon olive oil

Salt and freshly ground
   pepper

1 tablespoon fresh thyme

4 slices whole wheat bread,
   toasted

1. Preheat the oven to 400 degrees.

2. Remove the fennel stalks and reserve 2 table-spoons fennel fronds. Cut the fennel bulb in half, remove the core, and chop the remaining fennel.

3. In a small saucepan, bring 1 cup water to a boil. Add the chopped fennel, onion, shallots, and cardamom. Cover and cook for 15 minutes or until the vegetables are tender.

4. Pat the flounder fillets dry and spread a small amount of tapenade on both sides.

5. Pour the vermouth into a large skillet and add the fillets. Drizzle with the olive oil and bring to a boil over medium heat. Place the skillet in the oven and cook for 10 to 15 minutes.

6. Meanwhile, transfer the fennel, onion, and shallot mixture to a blender and purée. Season to taste and stir in half of the thyme.

7. Remove the skillet from the oven and transfer the fish to a plate and keep warm. Place the skillet over medium heat and bring the cooking liquid to a boil for 1 to 2 minutes to thicken slightly.

8. To serve, place one slice of toasted bread, spread with the fennel purée, on the plate and top with 1 fillet. Spoon the pan sauce on top of the fish and around the plate, add the remaining thyme, and serve immediately.

JOHN DORY WITH TOMATOES AND CAPERS

¼ cup olive oil plus
  additional for garnish

2 (14.5-ounce) cans diced
  tomatoes

2 tablespoons capers in
  vinegar, drained

Salt and freshly ground
  pepper

4 (6-ounce) John Dory
  fillets (or use cod,
  monkfish, or halibut)

4 tablespoons fresh basil
  leaves cut into chiffonade
  (thin strips)

1. Preheat the oven to 400 degrees.

2. Heat ¼ cup olive oil in a medium saucepan over medium heat and add the tomatoes and capers. Season to taste and simmer for 5 minutes.

3. Place half of the tomato-caper mixture in a baking dish, add the fillets, and cover with the remaining tomato-caper mixture. Bake until the fish is cooked through, 15 to 20 minutes.

4. To serve, place 1 fillet on each plate and spoon the sauce over. Garnish with basil and a drizzle of olive oil.

And a Little Meat

A little protein at lunch is essential (there's always a few nuts!), and instead of putting slabs of protein between two slices of bread, why not consume it hot or cold in a quick and easy preparation? The argument I made for fish at lunch mostly holds for the meat dishes that follow. Short of eating raw meat, I cannot think of any simpler meat preparation than sautéing thin veal cutlets—as in perhaps three minutes from refrigerator to plate. And cooked chicken, of course, can be refrigerated and enjoyed for a few days, including shredded in a salad. Eating something green along with your meat is always a good idea. And, oh, if you really miss your sandwich bread, have a slice of multigrain bread with your small portion of meat.

VEAL SCALOPPINE
À LA MOUTARDE

• SERVES 4 •

4 (3- to 4-ounce) veal cutlets, pounded thin

2½ tablespoons whole grain mustard

1 tablespoon olive oil

1 tablespoon butter

1. Pat the veal cutlets dry with paper towels and spread both sides with mustard.

2. In a large skillet, heat the olive oil and butter over medium heat. Add the veal and cook until golden, 3 to 5 minutes on each side. Serve immediately.

NOTE: *This works as well with chicken breast or turkey white meat, pounded thin.*

SAUTÉ OF TURKEY
WITH SPRING VEGETABLES

• SERVES 4 •

4 turkey cutlets, pounded
   thin
2 tablespoons paprika
Salt and freshly ground
   pepper
4 tablespoons olive oil
4 small onions, peeled and
   thinly sliced
2 cups frozen peas
2 cups frozen snow peas
1 cup heavy cream
2 tablespoons finely chopped
   fresh cilantro

1. Season both sides of the turkey cutlets with the paprika and salt and pepper.

2. Heat 2 tablespoons olive oil in a large skillet over medium-high heat and add the turkey cutlets. Cook until lightly golden, 3 to 4 minutes per side. Transfer the cutlets to a plate and keep warm.

3. Heat the remaining 2 tablespoons olive oil in the skillet and add the onions. Sauté until soft, about 4 minutes. Add the peas and snow peas and sauté until warm, about 1 minute. Add the cream and simmer until slightly thickened, about 4 minutes.

4. Add the turkey cutlets back to the pan, correct the seasoning, and add the cilantro. Cook for another 2 minutes and serve immediately.

CHICKEN WITH SPINACH
EN PAPILLOTE

• SERVES 4 •

1 tablespoon olive oil

4 generous cups fresh
  spinach, washed and
  dried

Salt and freshly ground
  pepper

2 tablespoons lemon juice

4 (6- to 8-ounce) skinless,
  boneless chicken breasts

4 bay leaves

2 cups cherry tomatoes

1 cup bulgur, cooked
  according to package
  instructions

1. Preheat the oven to 400 degrees.

2. Cut four pieces of parchment paper into 12- x 16-inch rectangles. Place them, stacked on top of one another, horizontally on a clean work surface. Beginning with the top sheet, brush the center with olive oil and top with 1 generous cup of spinach. Season to taste and sprinkle with ½ tablespoon lemon juice. Place 1 chicken breast, seasoned with salt and pepper, on the bed of spinach and top with 1 bay leaf and ½ cup cherry tomatoes. Seal the packet by bringing up the sides to the center and folding down together tightly. Tuck the top and bottom ends underneath and repeat with the remaining ingredients, creating 4 packets.

3. Place the packets on a baking sheet and bake in a preheated oven for 35 to 40 minutes. Remove from the oven and set one packet on each plate. Carefully open and remove the bay leaf. Spoon some cooked bulgur on top and serve immediately.

CARAMELIZED CHICKEN WITH VEGETABLE "PANCAKE"

• SERVES 4 •

1 carrot, washed and grated

2 medium potatoes, peeled and grated

1 small zucchini, washed and grated

1 garlic clove, peeled and minced

½ teaspoon fresh thyme

3 tablespoons olive oil

Salt and freshly ground pepper

FOR THE VEGETABLE PANCAKE

1. Place the grated carrot, potatoes, and zucchini in the center of a large, clean kitchen towel. Wrap tightly and squeeze as much liquid as possible from the vegetables. Unroll and place the grated vegetables in a large bowl. Add the garlic, thyme, and 1 tablespoon olive oil and mix well.

2. In a large, nonstick sauté pan, heat the remaining 2 tablespoons olive oil over medium-high heat. Add the vegetable mixture to the pan, pressing down so the pancake is about ½ inch thick and cook until golden brown, about 8 minutes. Carefully flip the pancake over (you can invert onto a plate first and slide back into the pan if you are nervous about the pancake falling apart) and continue cooking until the other side is crisp and golden and the vegetables are cooked, another 8 to 10 minutes. Remove from the pan and keep warm. Season to taste.

1 lemon, rinsed, dried, and
    quartered

12 small green olives, pitted
    and cut in half

½ teaspoon hot red pepper
    flakes

2 tablespoons honey

1 tablespoon lemon juice

3 tablespoons olive oil

4 (6- to 8-ounce) skinless,
    boneless chicken breasts

Salt and freshly ground
    pepper

FOR THE CARAMELIZED CHICKEN

1. In a large bowl, combine the lemon, olives, red pepper flakes, honey, lemon juice, and 1 tablespoon olive oil. Add the chicken breasts, season to taste, and stir to coat.

2. Heat the remaining 2 tablespoons olive oil in a large sauté pan over medium-high heat. Add the chicken-lemon-olive mixture and sauté until the chicken is cooked through and slightly caramelized, about 8 minutes per side. Serve the chicken with lemon and olives and accompanied by a wedge of the vegetable pancake.

CURRIED CHICKEN
WITH CUCUMBER

• SERVES 4 •

1 tablespoon unsalted butter

1 tablespoon olive oil

4 (6- to 8-ounce) skinless, boneless chicken breasts, cut lengthwise into ½-inch strips

Salt and freshly ground pepper

½ cup crème fraîche

1 tablespoon curry powder

2 seedless cucumbers, washed and cut into ½-inch slices

Juice of 1 lemon

Cooked basmati rice for serving

1. Heat the butter and olive oil in a large skillet over medium-high heat. Season the chicken with salt and pepper and add to the skillet. Cook until golden, stirring occasionally, about 10 minutes.

2. Meanwhile, in a medium bowl, combine the crème fraîche, curry, and cucumber slices and set aside.

3. When the chicken is golden, deglaze the pan with the lemon juice, scraping up all the brown bits from the bottom of the pan. Add the cucumber mixture and stir to combine. Cook for about 3 minutes or until the cucumbers are al dente. Season to taste and serve with basmati rice.

Chapter Three

DINNER

À TABLE

*D*inner hour is a puzzle and a wonder. What time do you normally eat dinner? Does it leave a healthy pause before going to bed? Do you tend to eat a big, bigger, and biggest dinner? How does dinner correlate with your health and with your sleep patterns? For every study and piece of advice I've read or heard, I can point to exceptions that seem to work just fine.

This much I know for myself: the older I get, the earlier and lighter I prefer to eat dinner. Now I can dine at 7:15 or 7:30 PM, compared with the 8:30 PM of most of my years. And the lighter my dinner is, the better I sleep and the better I feel the next morning. That said, in France where I live a good part of the year, try to get a dinner reservation in a restaurant before 8 PM. The French dine at 8:30 or 9 PM. Go to a restaurant that takes an

earlier reservation and when the French show up and see people already with dessert, they say to themselves and sometimes out loud, "tourists." And by the way, in France and Germany and the rest of Europe of the same latitude or higher, from mid-spring through summer and mid-fall, the hours of daylight are far longer than Americans appreciate. Daylight at 9 PM is routine and surely affects the dining hour.

I remember well a different picture during a stay in Bilbao, Spain, when jet-lagged and starving, the earliest reservation we could get for dinner at a top restaurant was 8:30 PM. We arrived at an empty restaurant and ate our entire meal with just one other couple in the dining room. Then as we were getting ready to leave, the Spaniards, legendary for dining late, started to flock in. I always wonder how they can eat and drink so well, so late, and then go to work and function first thing in the morning. Same in Greece. Go figure. In New York in the excess days of the 1980s and 1990s, I recall the poshest restaurants would keep their kitchens open past midnight and take full dinner orders until 11 PM to accommodate the arrival of a wealthy South American crowd around 10:30 PM (and thereby permitting the restaurant to turn tables three times in an evening, starting at about 5:30 or 6 PM when they would open their doors for pretheater dinner).

And there is the other extreme. The classic factory worker or physical laborer who comes home depleted and wants and expects dinner on the table shortly thereafter. That surely was the industrial and agrarian age standard and fully understandable, even necessary. And that time fix lingers on. But many of us no longer work long hours toiling in the fields and don't need to refuel our bodies depleted of its reserves so urgently or robustly. In the world's most populous country, China, dinner is relatively early, in my experience 6:30 or 7 PM, even for the fanciest state banquets, which are generally concluded by 9 PM or earlier. In a world homogenized by globalization, it seems dinner customs are slow to change, but they are indeed evolving.

Growing up French, I had the luxury of eating lunch always as the main meal of the day and considered it dinner. Schools and businesses closed from noon to two o'clock (well, fourteen o'clock in Europe) and we sat down at the table 12:30 sharp and did not get up until 1:30 PM. Both my parents worked, and the weekday meals were somewhat formulaic: fish every Friday, steak every Wednesday. Always a main protein dish, two vegetables (usually a type and style of potato was one), a simple green salad, and dessert in the form of fruit unless mother had to make us eat "horse steak," and then a more elaborate dessert was de rigueur as the bargaining power oh so subtly presented to encourage me to eat my steak. (My mother was great at planning—whether shopping the day before or preparing the basics for lunch before work, she was on top of things. It is a wonder how she did it all.)

Starting at age six, my job was to set the table. My father's job year-round was to go to the garden to pick the salad greens and fresh herbs after he had tenderly kissed my mother on her neck while she was attending the stove and putting the final touches to her cooking. The laughter and conversation around the "lunch" table is one of my strongest and best memories of childhood. The food wasn't bad either. The tone and warmth of all the wordplay and punning and silly jokes is hard to forget. (My father would say to me, "How do you make a golden soup?" "Add fourteen carrots.") Following a big lunch, dinner then was "supper," usually a soup (warm and rich in the winter, cold and light in the summer), perhaps some charcuterie such as ham, salami, or pâté, or an omelet, a salad, some cheese, mostly "creamy" such as *fromage blanc* or *petit-suisse*. No baked desserts at supper, only fruit. Dinner was lunchtime on weekends as well, but that was when my mother exercised her cooking skills and passion. It was a *menu dégustation* of sorts with a couple of *amuse* before the *plat de résistance*. The cheese tray was a treat served with wonderful breads. We always had guests and my mother always baked a dessert *and fruit tarts were the predessert!* Also it was the one day (or two) a week when we were permitted French fries!

That dining way of life is increasingly less the practice in France or in our world, though in the warmest climates and in the South of France, for example, shops still close for a long stretch at midday and people go home for a meal and a nap. One advantage of the midday main meal, I've come to realize, is that we get up and go about and the physical activity after lunch allows calories to burn faster and longer at an accelerated pace. It also means not a heavy consumption of alcohol near bedtime, which has the tendency to affect sleep patterns, causing us to awaken in the middle of the night, often dehydrated.

In Paris, my friend Agathe is more the sign of contemporary urban times and has adapted to her married life, and as a young wife who works long hours (and so does her husband, Gilles) her "married" eating pattern is as follows: breakfast is early and a moment where the couple sits down for a few minutes together before going their own way for the day. For both it's a piece of toast with butter and jam (made by Agathe's mother) with a yogurt and a cup of black coffee. Lunch in her case is a salad (sometimes bought in a good little shop near the Madeleine where she works or more often than not prepared by her at home and typically will be greens with seasonal color—tomatoes or carrots, some protein such as a boiled egg or a few olives, lots of herbs and a lemon juice–olive oil dressing) and a piece of fruit. She has an hour for lunch but will take half of it to eat and the other half to walk and shop in the neighborhood and often run errands. Dinner is late, about 9 PM, and since they both love to cook, they share the work each week; he does two days, she does two, and midweek they eat in a simple *bon rapport qualité-prix* (good value) bistro in their neighborhood. Their meals consist mostly of fish with vegetables, a glass or two of wine, and a fruit for dessert, except for the night out when they'll share a dessert. Weekends go in reverse, and they'll get together with friends; the main meal will tend to be lunch on Sunday. In Europe, Sunday lunch is still the regimented meal for family and friends, especially mothers-in-law.

So, what is the point of these observations? It is to "know thyself," and as a function of your lifestyle find the right and healthy balance of time and quantity, then embrace what is a good dinner for you. Dinner comes in all sizes and times, so learn to eat with your head and you will find a winning way. Here's my "contemporary" definition of dinner: the main meal of the day when you sit at a table with knife and fork and eat slowly. *À table, bien sûr.*

One more bit of advice—and forgive me for a true but "self-flattering" portion control story. A friend shared the following: she was eating dinner with her husband in a relatively high-end Manhattan restaurant and two young couples sat next to them. They appeared to be enjoying a special occasion, and the guys ate and drank more than their share. At dessert time they were sent a free extra dessert in addition to the one each had ordered for him or herself. The young women then declared: "Wow, what would Mireille do if she were here?" Well today, I would not finish the desserts, and I would walk away toward home before hailing a taxi. But I confess, in my twenties, I would have eaten the desserts. Nature has a way of forgiving our youthful ways. In our twenty-first-century increasingly urban and pressured society, people tend to overeat at dinner and binge on weekends. So, if a little Mireille in your head can serve as your portion-control and balance conscience, I'm happy.

Soups

BUTTERNUT SQUASH SOUP

• SERVES 4 TO 6 •

1 medium (2 to 2½ pounds) butternut squash, peeled, halved, seeds and strings discarded

2 tablespoons olive oil

2 tablespoons unsalted butter

1 large white onion, roughly chopped

2 garlic cloves, peeled and chopped

½ teaspoon freshly grated nutmeg

3 sprigs fresh thyme

3 fresh sage leaves plus additional for garnish

3 carrots, peeled and roughly chopped

1 Granny Smith apple, peeled, cored, and chopped

4 to 5 cups chicken broth

Salt and freshly ground pepper

1. Cut the butternut squash into 1-inch pieces and set aside.

2. In a large pot, heat the oil and butter over medium-high heat. Add the onion and garlic and sauté until fragrant and softened, about 4 minutes. Add the nutmeg, thyme, and sage and cook for another minute, stirring. Add the squash, carrots, apple, and 4 cups chicken broth. Bring to a boil, lower the heat, and cover. Simmer until the vegetables are tender, about 20 minutes.

3. Remove the thyme sprigs and sage leaves from the soup and carefully transfer the mixture to a blender or a food mill and purée until smooth. If a thinner consistency is desired, add the remaining 1 cup chicken broth. Season to taste and serve hot.

NOTE: *Sage leaves quickly fried in butter are a brilliant complement to the soup's natural sweetness. To prepare, simply melt 3 tablespoons butter in a small sauté pan over medium heat, swirling the pan occasionally. Add whole sage leaves and sauté until brown and toasted, 1 to 2 minutes. Garnish each serving of soup with 1 or 2 leaves and a drizzle of butter.*

POTAGE D'HIVER
(WINTER SOUP)

1 pound potatoes, peeled
and cut into 1-inch pieces

½ pound carrots, peeled and
sliced

½ pound leeks, white parts
only, washed and sliced

Salt and freshly ground
pepper

2 tablespoons finely chopped
fresh parsley

1. Place the potatoes, carrots, and leeks in a large pot and add water to cover. Bring to a boil, reduce the heat to medium-low, and cover. Simmer until the vegetables are tender, about 20 minutes.

2. Remove from the heat and carefully pour the vegetables into a food mill or blender and purée, adding the cooking liquid until the desired consistency is attained. Be sure not to overblend as the starch in the potatoes can make the soup's consistency become "gluey." Season to taste, garnish with parsley, and serve hot.

LENTIL AND CELERIAC SOUP

1 tablespoon olive oil

1 onion, peeled and chopped

1 garlic clove, peeled and
  chopped

1¼ cups green lentils

1 small celeriac, peeled and
  chopped

6 cups water or chicken stock

Drizzle of red wine vinegar

1 tablespoon crème fraîche

Salt and freshly ground
  pepper

1. Heat the olive oil in a large saucepan over medium heat. Add the onion and garlic and sauté until fragrant and softened, 3 to 4 minutes.

2. Add the lentils, celeriac, and water or chicken stock. Bring to a boil, cover and simmer until the lentils are tender, about 20 minutes. Carefully transfer the mixture to a food processor or food mill and purée until smooth and creamy.

3. Stir in the vinegar to taste and crème fraîche, season to taste, and serve hot.

PUMPKIN AND APPLE SOUP

· SERVES 4 TO 6 ·

2 tablespoons olive oil

1 medium onion, peeled and
   chopped

2 teaspoons peeled and
   finely grated fresh ginger

2 to 3 pounds pumpkin,
   peeled, seeded, and
   chopped

2 Granny Smith apples,
   peeled, cored, and diced
   (about 1½ cups)

1 tablespoon honey

Pinch of cinnamon

Pinch of ground cloves

4 cups vegetable broth

Salt and freshly ground
   pepper

4 sprigs fresh rosemary

1. Warm the olive oil in a large pot over medium heat. Add the onion and ginger and sauté until softened, about 5 minutes.

2. Add the pumpkin, 1¼ cups diced apple, the honey, cinnamon, and ground cloves and cook, stirring for 1 minute. Add the vegetable broth and simmer for 10 minutes.

3. Carefully transfer the mixture to a food mill or blender and purée until smooth. Season to taste and serve the soup garnished with the remaining ¼ cup diced apple and sprigs of rosemary.

CREAM OF CELERIAC WITH PEAR AND BLUE CHEESE

• SERVES 4 TO 6 •

1½ pounds celeriac, peeled and chopped

2 Comice pears, peeled, cored, and chopped

4 cups chicken broth

⅔ cup crème fraîche

Salt and freshly ground pepper

4 tablespoons finely minced fresh chives

2 ounces blue cheese, crumbled, at room temperature

1. Place the celeriac, pears, and chicken broth in a large pot over medium-high heat and bring to a boil. Cover, reduce the heat, and simmer until the celeriac is tender, about 15 minutes.

2. Meanwhile, using a stand or hand mixer, whip the crème fraîche until soft peaks form. Season to taste and fold in the chives. Cover and refrigerate.

3. Carefully transfer the celeriac, pears, and chicken broth to a blender and purée until smooth. To serve, pour the hot soup into bowls and garnish with the crumbled blue cheese and whipped crème fraîche.

Pasta, Perché No?

ORECCHIETTE WITH BROCCOLI RABE AND SAUSAGE

• SERVES 4 •

10 ounces orecchiette

1 pound broccoli rabe, stems trimmed and roughly chopped

2 tablespoons olive oil

1 garlic clove, peeled and minced

1 small onion, peeled and finely chopped

½ pound hot Italian sausage, split lengthwise down the middle and removed from casings

1 cup tomato sauce

Salt and freshly ground pepper

⅓ cup grated pecorino

⅓ cup grated Parmesan

2 tablespoons minced fresh parsley

1. Cook the orecchiette in a large pot of boiling salted water until they begin to soften, about 8 minutes. Add the broccoli rabe and cook until the pasta is just tender but still firm to the bite (al dente), about 3 minutes. Drain and reserve.

2. While the pasta is cooking, heat the olive oil in a large sauté pan over medium heat. Add the garlic and onion and cook until fragrant and softened, about 3 minutes. Add the sausage, breaking it up with a wooden spoon, and cook until browned, 5 to 8 minutes.

3. Add the cooked pasta and broccoli rabe to the sauté pan and toss until fully incorporated. Stir in the tomato sauce and cook for 1 to 2 minutes until heated through. Taste and correct the seasonings. Sprinkle with the grated cheeses and parsley and serve immediately.

SPAGHETTI CARBONARA

• SERVES 4 •

· ·

You will find two spaghetti carbonara recipes that follow, and I like them both because they have brought hours of heated discussions on what to put or not to put in the carbonara. And discussed with Italian, French, American, or Spanish friends, no one agrees. Cream is a big debate. So is the cheese: pecorino or Parmesan or both. The brand of spaghetti and fresh versus packaged. What size do you cut the pancetta? When and how do you add the egg yolks? The amount of water in the pot (the Italians put too much, and I put the minimum and it works). And on and on. Here is one of my favorites, though as a French woman I like Edward's because of the cream, which many Italians consider blasphemy, though quite a few have loved it when we served it to them, but then they were eating it in New York and not in Italy. So when in Rome, you know what you have to do.

12 ounces spaghetti

2 medium eggs plus yolk of a third medium egg, beaten

¾ cup freshly grated Parmesan

¼ cup freshly grated pecorino

Salt and freshly ground pepper

1 teaspoon olive oil

¼ to ½ pound bacon, cut crosswise into ½-inch pieces or ¼-inch cubes (or 5 ounces pancetta, chopped)

1. Bring a large pot of salted water to a boil over high heat. Add the spaghetti and cook until al dente, about 8 minutes. While the pasta is cooking, whisk the eggs and egg yolk with the Parmesan and pecorino in a medium bowl. Season to taste and set aside.

2. Warm the olive oil in a large sauté pan over medium-high heat. Add the bacon and cook until lightly browned and the fat has rendered. If there seems to be an excessive amount of fat, remove a bit, reserving 4 to 5 tablespoons in the pan. Reduce the heat to low, add the garlic, and quickly sauté until fragrant, being careful not to brown it, about 45 seconds.

2 *garlic cloves, minced*

1 *tablespoon finely chopped*
fresh parsley

3. Drain the spaghetti and reserve ¼ cup of the cooking water. Slowly whisk in half of the reserved cooking water to warm the egg and cheese mixture.

4. Add the hot spaghetti to the skillet with bacon and toss well over medium heat. Remove the pan from the heat, add the egg mixture, and toss quickly until the pasta is evenly coated and the sauce has thickened, about 1 minute. If the sauce is too thick, thin with some of the reserved pasta cooking water. Divide the pasta among four plates, season to taste, and garnish with parsley.

SPAGHETTI CARBONARA
ALLA EDOARDO

• SERVES 4 •

I never stayed in the kitchen when Edward prepared his version, until I had to for this book, as I needed the specific amounts of ingredients. What amazes me and amuses me the most when he makes this dish is the state of the kitchen—almost as if a hurricane had gone through. But then we sit down and savor it with a great glass of Brunello di Montalcino, truly a cherished pleasure I will never tire of.

12 ounces spaghetti

2 medium eggs plus yolk of a third medium egg

⅔ cup heavy cream

⅔ cup freshly grated Parmesan

1 teaspoon olive oil

Sliver of butter (about ½ teaspoon)

5 ounces pancetta, diced in ¾-inch-long and ¼-inch-wide pieces

Freshly ground pepper

1. Bring 3 quarts of water to a boil in a heavy pot over high heat. Add a pinch of salt and the spaghetti. Cook for 8 minutes or until al dente. While the pasta is cooking, whisk the eggs, egg yolk, heavy cream, and Parmesan in a bowl until combined.

2. Heat a large, heavy skillet over medium heat and add the olive oil and butter, and sprinkle with the pancetta pieces. Cook until the pancetta is lightly colored, 3 to 4 minutes, and some of the fat has been rendered; the pancetta should remain soft. (Drain off some of the fat if there seems to be an excessive amount.)

Pinch of piment d'Espelette
  (available at gourmet
  stores) or red pepper
  flakes for a stronger
  flavor
2 tablespoons finely chopped
  fresh parsley

3. Drain the pasta and reserve ¼ cup of the cooking water. Add the spaghetti to the skillet with the pancetta. Mix gently over medium heat, shaking the pan for a minute or so. Add the egg mixture and toss until well incorporated, coating the pasta but not scrambling the eggs. Thin the sauce with the reserved water if necessary. Season to taste with a good dose of pepper and a pinch of *piment d'Espelette,* a mild pepper from Spain, and garnish with parsley. Serve *pronto*.

MACARONI WITH RICOTTA AND WALNUTS

10 ounces macaroni

1¼ cups walnuts, coarsely chopped

½ cup fresh basil leaves cut into chiffonade (thin strips)

1¼ cups fresh ricotta

½ cup freshly grated Parmesan

Salt and freshly ground pepper

1 to 2 tablespoons walnut oil

1. Bring a large pot of salted water to a boil. Add the macaroni and cook until al dente, 8 to 10 minutes.

2. Meanwhile, combine the walnuts, basil, ricotta, and Parmesan in a bowl and season to taste.

3. To serve, drain the cooked pasta and place in a serving bowl with the walnut oil, tossing well. Add the ricotta mixture to the pasta and toss to combine. Serve hot or at room temperature.

TAGLIATELLE WITH TURKEY "BOLOGNESE"

• SERVES 4 •

2 tablespoons olive oil

2 celery stalks, rinsed and diced

2 carrots, peeled and finely diced

½ large onion, peeled and finely chopped

2 garlic cloves, peeled and minced

1 teaspoon minced fresh rosemary

Pinch of paprika

1 boneless, skinless turkey breast half (about 8 ounces), diced

½ cup red wine

1 (14.5-ounce) can chopped tomatoes

12 ounces tagliatelle

¾ cup freshly grated pecorino

1. Heat the olive oil over medium heat in a large, heavy saucepan and add the celery, carrots, onion, garlic, rosemary, and paprika. Sauté, stirring occasionally, until softened and fragrant, about 4 minutes. Add the diced turkey and sauté until golden, 2 to 3 minutes.

2. Add the red wine and tomatoes, stirring to scrape any browned bits at the bottom of the pot. Cover, reduce the heat to medium-low, and cook for 30 minutes, stirring occasionally and adding a bit of water if the sauce becomes too dry.

3. While the sauce is simmering, bring a large pot of salted water to a boil. Add the tagliatelle and cook until al dente, about 10 minutes.

4. Drain the pasta and serve with the sauce, garnished with the pecorino.

Adding the Colors of Vegetables

POTATO AND FENNEL PURÉE

• SERVES 4 •

2 large fennel bulbs

4 medium potatoes, peeled and chopped

4 tablespoons olive oil plus extra for serving

⅓ cup chicken broth

Salt and freshly ground pepper

1 tablespoon minced fresh dill

1. Remove the stalks from each fennel bulb and reserve 1 tablespoon fronds. Remove the outer "envelopes" of each fennel bulb, slice in half to create cups, rinse, and reserve. Discard the stalks and core and chop the remaining fennel.

2. Place the fennel cups, chopped fennel, and potatoes in a steamer insert set over simmering water and cook for 20 minutes or until tender.

3. Remove the fennel cups and reserve. In a blender, combine the olive oil, chicken broth, and steamed chopped fennel, and purée until smooth. Pass the steamed potatoes through the fine plate of a ricer or food mill into a large bowl and add the fennel purée. Stir until smooth and season with salt and pepper.

4. Place one fennel cup on each plate, season with salt and pepper, and fill with the purée. Garnish with fresh dill, fennel fronds, and a drizzle of olive oil and serve.

QUINOA WITH PEAS AND FAVAS

1 cup quinoa

½ pound peas, fresh or
   frozen

½ pound fava beans, peeled

¾ cup snow peas, chopped

2½ tablespoons unsalted
   butter

1 tablespoon olive oil

½ teaspoon ground cumin

½ teaspoon ground
   coriander

Salt and freshly ground
   pepper

1. Cook the quinoa according to the package directions.

2. Meanwhile, place the vegetables and beans in a steamer and steam over medium to high heat until crisp-tender and bright green, 8 to 10 minutes. Be careful not to overcook.

3. Place the cooked quinoa in a serving bowl, add the butter, and mix well. Add the vegetables, olive oil, cumin, and coriander and season to taste. Serve hot or at room temperature.

CAULIFLOWER PURÉE

• SERVES 4 •

· ·

2½ cups chicken or vegetable broth

1 head cauliflower, stems and stalks trimmed, florets chopped (4 to 5 cups)

1 tablespoon unsalted butter

2 tablespoons sour cream (or fromage blanc)

1 tablespoon grated Parmesan

Pinch of paprika

Salt and freshly ground pepper

1. In a large saucepan, bring the chicken or vegetable broth to a boil over high heat. Add the cauliflower, cover, and simmer until very tender, about 12 minutes.

2. Reserve ¾ cup of the cooking liquid and carefully place half of the cauliflower in a blender. Add about ¼ cup of the cooking liquid and purée until smooth. Add the remaining cauliflower and blend, adding just enough liquid to produce a silky purée. Finish the purée by adding the butter, sour cream, Parmesan, and paprika and blending just until incorporated. Season to taste and serve hot.

POTATO RAGOÛT WITH PEPPERS, LEMON, AND OLIVES

• SERVES 4 •

5 tablespoons olive oil

2 large potatoes, peeled and
cut lengthwise into
quarters

1 red bell pepper, seeded
and cut into strips

4 garlic cloves, peeled and
minced

1 lemon, rinsed and sliced

1 cup green olives, pitted

Salt and freshly ground
pepper

½ cup fresh cilantro, finely
chopped

1. Preheat the oven to 375 degrees.

2. Heat 3 tablespoons olive oil in a large oven-safe skillet over medium heat. Add the potatoes, red pepper, and garlic and sauté until fragrant, about 2 minutes. Add the lemon slices and olives, season to taste, and place the skillet in the oven. Bake until the potatoes are golden and tender, 40 to 45 minutes.

3. Remove from the oven and transfer the vegetables to a serving bowl. Add the remaining 2 tablespoons olive oil and the fresh cilantro, gently toss to combine, and serve.

ROASTED CARROTS AND PUMPKIN WITH HERBS

1½ pounds small carrots, peeled and green tops trimmed to 1 to 3 inches

2 pounds pumpkin, peeled, seeded, and thinly sliced

Butter, softened, for baking dish

⅓ cup olive oil

1 garlic clove, peeled and minced

½ teaspoon ground cumin

½ teaspoon ground coriander

Salt and freshly ground pepper

2 tablespoons finely chopped fresh parsley

2 tablespoons finely chopped fresh mint

1. Preheat the oven to 375 degrees.

2. Place the carrots and pumpkin in a buttered baking dish. Add the olive oil, garlic, cumin, and coriander and toss to combine. Season to taste and place in the oven. Bake for about 40 minutes, stirring occasionally, until the vegetables are tender and very lightly caramelized.

3. Remove from the oven, sprinkle with parsley and mint, and serve.

SWEET POTATO FRENCH FRIES

• SERVES 4 •

Olive oil

4 medium sweet potatoes,
   unpeeled

Salt and freshly ground
   pepper

Sea salt for serving

1. Preheat the oven to 450 degrees and brush a baking sheet with olive oil.

2. Halve the sweet potatoes lengthwise and cut each half into 3 to 5 spears. Place the spears on the prepared baking sheet, season to taste, and bake, turning the spears once, for 15 to 20 minutes until crisp. Remove from the oven, sprinkle with sea salt, and serve hot.

MUSHROOMS AND SWISS CHARD

• SERVES 4 •

1 tablespoon olive oil

1 tablespoon unsalted butter

1 large shallot, peeled and
   minced

1 pound Swiss chard, center
   ribs discarded and leaves
   coarsely chopped

¾ pound mixed mushrooms
   (use a variety such as
   portobello, shiitake, and
   button), wiped clean and
   chopped

Salt and freshly ground
   pepper

1. Heat the olive oil and butter in a large skillet over medium-high heat. Add the shallot and sauté until fragrant and softened, 1 minute.

2. Add the Swiss chard and cook, stirring, until tender, 5 to 7 minutes. Add the mushrooms and sauté for 3 minutes. Season to taste and serve immediately.

NOTE: *In addition to being a delicious side dish, this makes a fabulous sandwich. Place a layer of mushrooms and Swiss chard on a slice of baguette or other good, crusty bread. Top with a few slices of fresh mozzarella and place under the broiler until melted. Sprinkle with salt and serve immediately.*

LEEKS MOZZARELLA

• SERVES 4 •

2 pounds leeks, white parts
   only
1 cup fresh basil leaves
8 ounces mozzarella
1 to 2 tablespoons olive oil
1 teaspoon wine or sherry
   vinegar
Salt, preferably freshly
   ground fleur de sel
   (large-grained "flower of
   salt" harvested from the
   sea works magic), and
   freshly ground pepper
4 slices country bread

1. Preheat the broiler.

2. Clean the leeks thoroughly and boil in salted water for 6 to 10 minutes, until cooked but still firm, then drain.

3. Put the leeks in a baking dish and cover with a layer of basil leaves. Cut the mozzarella into ¼-inch slices and place atop the basil layer. Put the dish under the preheated broiler and watch carefully. In 3 to 5 minutes the cheese should start to melt and brown; at this point, remove the dish.

4. Mix the oil and vinegar and drizzle over the mozzarella. Season with salt and pepper to taste. Serve immediately with a slice of country bread.

QUINOA AND BEET SALAD

· SERVES 4 TO 6 ·

2 tablespoons red wine
vinegar
2 tablespoons lemon juice
6 tablespoons olive oil
Salt and freshly ground
pepper
1 cup quinoa, cooked
according to the package
directions
1 pound red beets, boiled,
peeled, and quartered
½ pound mushrooms,
cleaned and minced
1 avocado, pitted, peeled,
and diced
2 yellow peppers, seeded,
sliced into thin strips,
and steamed
¼ cup red onion, peeled and
finely diced
2 tablespoons coarsely
chopped almonds
¼ cup chopped fresh parsley

1. In a small bowl combine the vinegar and lemon juice. Slowly drizzle in the olive oil while whisking and season to taste.

2. Place the quinoa in a large bowl and add the beets, mushrooms, avocado, yellow peppers, onion, and almonds. Pour the dressing over the salad and gently toss. Sprinkle with parsley and serve.

BLACK OLIVE POTATO SALAD
WITH FAVA BEANS

• SERVES 4 •

¾ pound Red Bliss potatoes,
  unpeeled

2 tablespoons black olive
  tapenade (store-bought)

3 tablespoons olive oil

Salt and freshly ground
  pepper

1 pound fava beans,
  shelled, peeled, cooked
  for 1 minute in boiling,
  salted water, and drained

½ cup sun-dried tomatoes,
  coarsely chopped

1. Place the potatoes in a pot of salted cold water. Bring to a boil and cook for 10 minutes or until a fork can easily pierce the potatoes. Drain and quarter.

2. Meanwhile, in a small bowl combine the tapenade and olive oil and season to taste.

3. Place the potatoes, fava beans, and sun-dried tomatoes in a large bowl. Pour the tapenade mixture over the salad, toss well, and serve at room temperature.

Omega-3 to the Rescue:
Toujours Poissons

SARDINES WITH CARROTS AND LEEKS

• SERVES 4 •

3 tablespoons olive oil

6 ounces carrots, peeled and thinly sliced

Salt and freshly ground pepper

10 ounces leeks, white parts only, thinly sliced

2 tablespoons minced shallots

1 tablespoon unsalted butter

12 medium fresh sardines (about 1½ pounds)

1 tablespoon minced fresh oregano

Juice of 1 lemon

1. Preheat the oven to 350 degrees.

2. Warm 2 tablespoons of the olive oil in a large skillet. Add the carrots and cook over medium heat for 5 minutes. Add ⅓ cup water, season to taste, and stir in the leeks and shallots. Cover and cook for 5 to 7 minutes, stirring occasionally, until the vegetables are tender. Add the butter and cook a minute or two more.

3. Put the sardines in one layer in a shallow 9- x 13-inch baking dish. Drizzle the remaining 1 tablespoon olive oil over them, season to taste, and sprinkle with oregano. Bake 5 to 7 minutes on each side. Drizzle with the lemon juice and serve with the carrots and leeks.

MACKEREL WITH CARROTS AND LEEKS

• SERVES 4 •

3 tablespoons olive oil

4 tablespoons minced fresh rosemary

2 tablespoons minced shallots

Juice of 1 lemon

1½ pounds mackerel fillets

Salt and freshly ground pepper

Carrot-leek mixture from Sardines with Carrots and Leeks (page 136)

1. Make a marinade by combining 2 tablespoons of the olive oil with the rosemary, shallots, and lemon juice. Pour over the mackerel and marinate for 10 to 20 minutes.

2. Warm the remaining tablespoon olive oil in a large skillet and cook the mackerel over medium heat, about 3 minutes on each side.

3. Season to taste (be careful not to oversalt, since mackerel is already salty) and serve with the carrot-leek mixture.

FRIED OYSTERS

• SERVES 4 •

Life is filled with surprises. I love oysters, and never imagined what I learned from my books, websites, and appearances: that so many people had never tasted oysters and/or did not want to taste oysters. (I'll spare you the adjectives describing those poor mollusks.) And also that so many people are allergic to shellfish and seafood, and for that I have compassion—you are missing one of the most sensual foods on earth or as Léon Paul Fargue said, "Eating oysters will always be like kissing the sea on the lips."

Here is an easy introduction to the oyster via a recipe (the only oyster recipe in this book). I truly hope a few more readers will be adventurous and taste oysters. I like oysters best raw, but what I've learned (similar lessons with Champagne, broccoli, and fish) is don't try the raw stuff first. Manipulate: coat it, "cajole" it, hide it. Since most of us like fried foods, and fried oysters are made quickly, here is one of my favorite "non raw" ways of eating oysters.

Vegetable oil, for frying

¾ cup flour

¾ cup cornmeal

1 egg, beaten

1 dozen oysters, opened, removed from shells, and patted dry

Salt

Lemon wedges or Quick "Aïoli," page 140 (optional)

1. Heat the oil in a deep, heavy saucepan over medium-high heat until the oil is 375 degrees; the oil should be at least 3 inches deep.

2. Meanwhile, place the flour and cornmeal on separate plates and place the egg in a small bowl. Dredge 1 oyster in the flour and shake off the excess. Dip in the egg, remove with a fork, and roll in cornmeal until well coated. Shake off any excess and set on a plate. Repeat with the remaining oysters.

3. When the oil is ready, carefully deep-fry the oysters, three at a time, until golden, about 2 minutes. Be sure to monitor the temperature of the oil: if the oysters brown too fast, reduce the heat, and if they cook too slowly, increase the heat. Carefully remove the oysters with a slotted spoon and set on a paper towel–lined plate. Sprinkle with salt and serve immediately with lemon wedges or aïoli, if desired.

QUICK "AÏOLI"

• MAKES 1 CUP •

* 1 cup good-quality
  mayonnaise
* 1 large garlic clove, peeled
  and finely minced
* 1 teaspoon lemon juice
* 1 tablespoon finely chopped
  fresh basil

Combine all the ingredients and serve.

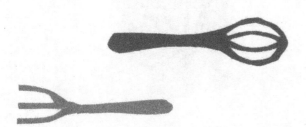

MACKEREL WITH CURRY
AND LEEKS

• SERVES 4 •

1 tablespoon olive oil

2 tablespoons unsalted
butter

1 pound leeks, washed
carefully to remove grit,
halved vertically, and cut
into thin strips

2 shallots, peeled and finely
chopped

1 pound potatoes, peeled,
washed, cut into ¼-inch
dice, and reserved in a
bowl of cold water

1 bouquet garni (a bundle or
small sachet of mixed
herbs)

1 teaspoon curry powder

4 (4-ounce) mackerel fillets

Salt and freshly ground
pepper

1. Preheat the oven to 400 degrees.

2. Heat the olive oil and 1 tablespoon butter in a
saucepan over medium-low heat and sauté the
leeks and shallots until fragrant and softened, 10
minutes.

3. Add the potatoes and just enough water to
cover them, along with the bouquet garni and
curry powder. Bring to a boil, cover, and cook
over medium to low heat for 10 to 12 minutes or
until the potatoes can be pierced with a fork.

4. Carefully pour the potatoes and cooking liquid
into a baking dish. Top with the mackerel fillets,
season to taste, and dot the fillets with the remaining tablespoon of butter. Bake for 15 minutes and
serve immediately from the baking dish.

FLOUNDER FILLETS WITH
PAPRIKA SAUCE

4 medium carrots, peeled

¼ pound haricots verts, trimmed

4 (4-ounce) flounder fillets (may also use snapper or sea bream)

2 tablespoons olive oil

Salt and freshly ground pepper

1 tablespoon butter

1⅓ cups heavy cream

2 teaspoons paprika

½ teaspoon sugar

2 tablespoons minced chives

1. Slice the carrots into matchsticks as long as the width of the fillets, about 3 inches. Cut the haricots verts to the same length.

2. Place the haricots verts in a steamer insert set above simmering water and steam for 2 minutes, covered. Add the carrots, cover, and steam for an additional 6 minutes or until crisp-tender. Remove from the heat and reserve.

3. Lay the fillets vertically on a work surface and pat dry. Brush the top of the fillets with 1 tablespoon olive oil and season to taste. Place one bundle of carrots and haricots verts at the bottom of a fillet and roll up, securing with a toothpick. Repeat with the other fillets.

4. Heat the butter and the remaining tablespoon olive oil over medium heat in a large skillet and add the fillets. Cover and cook for 4 to 6 minutes on each side.

5. Transfer the fillets to a plate and keep warm. Add the cream, paprika, and sugar to the skillet and whisk to combine. Increase the heat to medium-high and simmer until thickened, about 5 minutes. Remove from the heat, stir in the chives, and correct the seasoning.

6. Place each fillet on a plate, spoon the sauce over and around, and serve immediately.

TUNA WITH GREEN SAUCE

• SERVES 4 •

. . . .

One of the ways to increase your fish intake—at least one of the ways I increase mine—is to make two meals out of one-time cooking. Tuna and salmon in particular are two cooked fish I enjoy eating cold the next day or two as part of a salad. So, I tend to make steaklike fish for my evening meal, not only because they are bulkier and fall into the American pattern of lighter meals that culminate in a more substantial main meal at dinner but because I cook a small extra portion to supply the protein for my lunch salads. And while a cold fish is not my idea of dinner, it is quick and appealing for lunch.

½ cup fresh parsley, chopped

1 green pepper, rinsed, seeded, and chopped into ¼-inch dice

½ cup green olives, pitted and chopped

2 tablespoons capers, rinsed and drained

1 teaspoon fresh thyme

2 tablespoons olive oil

Juice of 1 lemon

⅔ cup white wine or dry vermouth

1 (1-pound) tuna steak, cut into 4 pieces

Salt and freshly ground pepper

1. Preheat the oven to 375 degrees.

2. In a bowl, combine the parsley, green pepper, olives, capers, thyme, 1 tablespoon olive oil, lemon juice, and wine. Pour into a baking dish, place in the oven, and bake for 10 minutes.

3. Lower the heat to 350 degrees. Remove the baking dish from the oven, add the tuna, spoon the sauce over, drizzle with the remaining tablespoon olive oil, and season to taste. Return the baking dish to the oven and cook for 10 to 15 minutes or until the tuna is done to taste. Remove from the oven and serve immediately.

Meat

PORK CHOPS WITH APPLES

• SERVES 4 •

· ·

4 medium pork chops

4 whole cloves

½ cup dry white wine or vermouth

4 celery leaves

2 bay leaves

4 celery stalks, washed and finely diced

1 tablespoon butter

2 apples, cored and coarsely sliced

1 tablespoon brown sugar

4 ounces Swiss or Jarlsberg cheese, coarsely grated

1. Preheat the oven to 375 degrees. Butter a baking pan and place the pork chops in it.

2. Press a clove into each chop. Add the white wine, celery leaves, and bay leaves and put the pan in the preheated oven. Bake the chops for 30 minutes.

3. While the pork chops are baking, in a frying pan, sauté the diced celery in the butter for 5 minutes, then add the sliced apples and sprinkle with the brown sugar. Continue cooking over very low heat for 10 minutes, or until the apples are tender but not mushy.

4. Finish the pork chops by removing the bay and celery leaves and sprinkle the cheese over the top of each chop; baste and then broil for a few minutes to brown the top.

5. Serve the celery-apple mixture on the plate as an accompaniment to the pork chops. Use a few spoons of the pan juices to further flavor the celery-apple mixture.

ROSEMARY LAMB MEATBALLS

• SERVES 4 TO 6 •

(MAKES ABOUT THIRTY 1¼-INCH MEATBALLS) •

· ·

4 slices whole wheat bread, crusts removed

1 pound ground lamb shoulder

1 medium onion, peeled, grated, and excess moisture removed

1 garlic clove, peeled and minced

2 tablespoons finely diced sun-dried tomatoes

2 tablespoons finely minced fresh rosemary

1 tablespoon olive oil plus additional for baking sheet

1 teaspoon quatre épices *

Salt and freshly ground pepper

Buttered noodles or cooked brown rice for serving

1. Preheat the oven to 425 degrees. Soak the bread in a small amount of water for 5 minutes. Firmly squeeze the bread to remove any excess water, discard the water, and place in a large bowl with the ground lamb. Add the onion, garlic, sun-dried tomatoes, rosemary, 1 tablespoon olive oil, and quatre épices. Season to taste and mix well.

2. To form the meatballs, wet your hands with cold water (to prevent sticking) and form 1¼-inch balls.

3. Arrange the meatballs on a large, heavy oiled baking sheet and bake until firm and cooked through, 12 to 15 minutes, turning once halfway.

4. Serve hot over buttered noodles or brown rice.

NOTE: *These meatballs would also be great made smaller, skewered, and served with mint-yogurt dip as an hors d'oeuvre, or make a delicious sandwich tucked inside a pita with chopped tomato and mint-yogurt dip. To make mint-yogurt dip, combine 2 cups plain Greek-style yogurt with ¼ cup finely chopped fresh mint and ½ cup peeled and grated cucumber, and season to taste.*

*Often used in France, quatre épices is a spice blend that usually consists of ground pepper, cloves, nutmeg, and ginger or cinnamon.

CHICKEN EN CROÛTE
FIONA STYLE

Zest of 2 lemons

Zest of 2 oranges

3 garlic cloves, peeled and minced

6 tablespoons minced fresh parsley

4 teaspoons minced fresh rosemary

1 cup grated Parmesan

2 teaspoons olive oil

Salt and freshly ground pepper

2 eggs

4 (5- to 6-ounce) skinless, boneless chicken breast halves, pounded to ⅓-inch thickness

1. Preheat the oven to 400 degrees. Cover a baking sheet with aluminum foil and set aside.

2. In a shallow bowl or pie plate, combine the zests, garlic, parsley, rosemary, Parmesan, and olive oil and season to taste. In a second shallow bowl, whisk the eggs with a pinch of salt.

3. Dip each chicken breast in the egg, allowing any excess to drip off, and then dip in the citrus-herb-Parmesan mixture, pressing to lightly coat each side. Place the chicken breasts on the prepared baking sheet and transfer to the oven. Bake for 20 minutes or until the chicken is done.

4. Remove from the oven and serve immediately with lemon slices and a green salad.

ITALIAN-STYLE CHICKEN

· SERVES 4 ·

1 tablespoon olive oil

4 (5- to 6-ounce) skinless,
    boneless chicken breasts,
    cut lengthwise into ½-
    inch strips

Salt and freshly ground
    pepper

¼ cup sun-dried tomatoes,
    soaked in hot water for
    10 minutes, drained, and
    chopped

8 black olives, pitted and
    quartered

1 tablespoon capers, rinsed
    and drained

Pinch of cayenne pepper

Sautéed spinach for serving

1. Heat the olive oil in a nonstick skillet over medium-high heat. Season the chicken pieces with salt and pepper and cook, stirring often, until golden, about 10 minutes. Remove the chicken from the pan and reserve.

2. Deglaze the pan with 2 tablespoons water and reduce until syrupy, about 1½ minutes. Add the tomatoes, olives, capers, and chicken and cook until heated through, about 1 minute. Correct the seasoning and add the cayenne. Serve immediately over spinach sautéed with garlic and lemon.

CHICKEN *À LA TUNISIENNE*

1 tablespoon butter

1 tablespoon olive oil

4 shallots, peeled and
   minced (about ½ cup)

1½ pounds boneless, skinless
   chicken breasts, cut into
   1-inch dice

1 (15-ounce) can apricots in
   their juice

½ teaspoon cinnamon

2 tablespoons crème fraîche

Salt and freshly ground
   pepper

Couscous for serving

1. Heat the butter and olive oil in a large, heavy saucepan over medium heat. Add the shallots and cook until softened, 2 to 3 minutes.

2. Add the chicken and cook, stirring, until the meat is golden. Stir in the apricots and their juice and the cinnamon. Cover, reduce the heat, and cook for 20 minutes. Remove the cover, increase the heat to medium-high and allow the cooking liquid to reduce slightly, about 10 minutes. Before serving, stir in the crème fraîche and season to taste. Serve with couscous.

CAREFREE CHICKEN

• SERVES 4 •

1 tablespoon olive oil

1 tablespoon unsalted butter

1 (3- to 4-pound) free-range chicken, cut into 6 pieces (2 breasts, 2 legs, 2 thighs), wings not included

1 large onion, peeled and minced

⅓ cup water

1 teaspoon curry powder

1 teaspoon ground cardamom

½ teaspoon freshly grated nutmeg

1 chicken bouillon cube

Pinch of paprika

1 cup canned tomatoes

Salt and freshly ground pepper

Rice for serving

1. Heat the olive oil and butter in a large skillet over medium-high heat. Add the chicken pieces and brown on all sides. Remove from the pan and reserve.

2. Using the same skillet, add the onion and cook until soft, 4 to 5 minutes. Deglaze the skillet with the water, scraping up any browned bits.

3. Add the curry powder, cardamom, nutmeg, bouillon cube, paprika, and tomatoes. Stir well and return the chicken pieces back to the skillet and season to taste. Cover and simmer over medium-low heat for 1 hour. Serve with basmati rice.

Chapter Four

EAT YOUR
FISH AND
VEGETABLES

*I*t's no secret that men and women have different tastes in food. In 2008 the results of the most extensive study of gender differences in eating habits found that men were more likely to eat meat and poultry, especially duck, beef, and ham. Women were more likely to eat vegetables, especially carrots and tomatoes, and fruits, especially strawberries, blueberries, raspberries, and apples. Women also preferred dry foods, such as almonds and walnuts, and were more likely to consume yogurt.

But just because men (or you) *tend* to favor steak over asparagus doesn't mean they can't learn to appreciate a delicious ratatouille or sardines with carrots and leeks, two of the most popular recipes in *French Women Don't Get Fat* and *French Women for All Seasons* respectively and reprinted in this book.

But first things first: you should eat more fish and vegetables. Short of over-dosing on mercury-toxic big fish (especially if you are pregnant), they are good for you. So, by design, I've included this chapter of additional fish and vegetable recipes to inspire readers to be adventurous and to tempt them to a path that marries health with happiness and pleasure. (*Ménage à trois?*) New dishes and preparations and presentations can mean new appeal and new habits, even new health. You probably know the reasons and recommendations for eating your fish and vegetables. The benefits of eating fish two to three times a week is to cover your protein (lunch or dinner) needs with food that is low in fat and high in good fat and antioxidants, which help reduce the risks of heart disease and al-leviate many conditions from inflammation to depression. In addition, fish is versatile in its varieties (shellfish, white fish, oily fish, etc.) and preparations (steam, bake, sauté, poach, *en papillote*, grill). As for vegetables, they are about the best food on the planet (nuts are competitors) and eating two to four por-tions a day is healthy to get your fiber, which fill the stomach but also because vegetables are low in fat like fish. The vitamins and minerals in vegetables are an energy booster, their low sodium content means less water retention and, of course, they, like fish, are loaded with antioxidants and protect against heart dis-ease, cancer, and much more. Along with water, the fibers in veggies (also in fruit and grains) act as a digestive tract stimulant. So, it was often said at our table when I was growing up "*Mange tes légumes,*" eat your veggies. Your me-tabolism will love it. As for preparations from raw to cooked, the ways are infi-nite and the mixing a true pleasure plus an easy way not to waste what's in the fridge.

Unless you are the rarity who dines all the time in restaurants (where you can order individually what you want) or you normally eat alone, you, like most people, dine with a companion or family members in a communal meal. Thus, you generally eat what is prepared for everyone *ensemble*. If your dining com-panions are "meat and potato" types, you may need to do a little missionary conversion. It is for your own good as well as theirs. Whether you are breaking poor eating habits, attempting to slim down, or just exploring a new culinary lifestyle, having co-explorers along to support you is a proven benefit. Having conscientious objectors along for the ride is proven not to be a good thing.

I converted my husband into a fish eater. It just took a little exposure and education. The conversion started during one of our very first "dates." I've written elsewhere how we met on a bus in Istanbul. That led to a reconnection in Athens, where we decided to go to the port of Piraeus for a fish dinner. The restaurant turned out to be literally out on a dock and ordering meant you walked into the area next to the kitchen and pointed to the fish you wanted to eat among dozens either still swimming in tanks or chilling on ice. Fresh as fresh can be. I'd spent quite a bit of time in Greece and spoke the language and knew the practice. There are Greek restaurants in New York that offer fish in the same wonderful manner. And top Chinese restaurants the world over do the same. For Edward, it was a revelation.

Though he had grown up a few miles from the ocean and ate fish every Friday in a Catholic household, he could not identify a single fish outside the goldfish bowl. Okay, I exaggerate, only slightly: he could identify mackerel and I expect swordfish (in a picture book). He had no idea what he was looking at in that seaside Greek restaurant. That evening he told me a story I have never forgotten.

Until he left for college, he mostly ate fish that looked and tasted like cardboard. So, it was no surprise he was shy on fish. It seems his mother only bought frozen fish (which meant to her fresh and no cleaning). He recalls blocks of frozen flounder fillet and now and then cod. Once they were thawed, she would mostly wash the fillets in egg batter, smother them in bread crumbs (from a can), and then panfry them in oil into an advanced state of rigor mortis. Occasionally a neighbor would deliver some freshly caught and cleaned fish, but then they, too, were inflicted with the same disguise and cooked to death. When he went off to college in New England, he occasionally tasted fish that were soft and tender, but mostly he acquired a taste for lobster.

So that evening in Piraeus, a whole fish, brushed with olive oil and lightly grilled to tender perfection, was an unusual treat and taste for him. Subsequently I (and my mother) used a little seductive French sauce as a "flavor enhancer" on delicately poached or broiled fish. Cooked tender and moist and not overdone. For him, it was like discovering a new food category. Correction: it was in fact discovering a new food category. And fish accompanied by potatoes or rice, what was not to like? Nowadays, I mostly avoid disguises, and twice a week at least we enjoy simply steamed or grilled fresh fish, and only sometimes with potatoes or rice, but always with something green (okay, once in a while orange or red).

If you need to convert a companion or children to diversify their meat and potatoes fixation, here are a few simple "tricks."

■ Effect a transition and remember balance. What if the kids want chicken fingers and French fries and you want them to eat fish? Don't shock them by serving salmon over a bed of spinach. Remember *peu à peu*, little by little. Serve a small portion of salmon with their favorite side dish, even if it's French fries. It may not be the perfect combo in your mind, but you'll have a much better chance of persuading picky eaters to eat something new if it's sitting next to something they enjoy. And you don't have to eat more than a few French fries yourself (hard, I know, but this is only the first half of the transition).

■ Add one vegetable at a time. Start by making a vegetable phobic try (just try) one green at dinner, or one new vegetable. Learn what flavor combinations your dining companion(s) like and serve the veggies that way. My friend and associate Erin learned that her meat-and-potatoes fiancé loved lemon-butter-garlic sauce. So she started introducing things he'd usually turn his nose up at (broccoli rabe, asparagus, zucchini) in lemon and butter with chopped garlic. It was a big hit. Soon he was not only happily scarfing down loads of greens, he was requesting them for dinner! Little by little she started reducing the amount of butter as his palate developed a taste for greens. She now only uses olive oil (no butter) and he never even knew the difference.

■ Create "secret" vegetable delivery systems (SVDS?). Soup is the time-tested secret of the French and the most efficient way to get vegetables into a finicky eater's diet. When made from scratch, soup is generally low in calories, high in water, and bursting with nutrients, not to mention a great first course. Omelets filled with veggies are another option. Serve with a small salad and/or potatoes. This is another great alternative for hungry men who usually go for bacon and eggs on Saturday mornings.

You can modify eating habits little by little. The key is to find a way to present new and healthy foods in a fun and delicious manner. Mothers of children who refuse to eat vegetables and fruits would be thrilled to know that another recent study found that when salad bars were placed in school lunchrooms, students took advantage, doubling their daily fresh produce intake. This "proves that kids will indeed eat more fruits and vegetables if offered in an appetizing and accessible manner" remarked the head of the study. I agree. You may not see improvement or acceptance at first; remember this is a process that will take a bit of time. And though you may get resistance, it doesn't mean the message is not sinking in. Maria, a community member on my website, shared with me, "I've always been one to prepare and enjoy good meals. For many years my daughter said everything was 'too fancy, too weird, too spicy, too something.' Who is the epicurean now? My daughter has a palate and natural talent for cooking that equals most foodies I know. It really seems that what she saw, as opposed to what she agreed to eat, as a child prevailed. Also, both my husband and his brother went through similar stages and are both refined eaters now." So remember, take the complaints in stride, stick to your guns, and, above all, remember to have patience. Good things often take time.

My additional fish dishes are all cooked *en papillote* because to me it's the most versatile way of serving fish: You have the choice to prepare it ahead (great time saver whether for a family meal or entertaining), it cooks fast and is foolproof (no worry to have under or overdone fish), you add your veggies in the package, it saves use and cleaning of another pot (you actually have no dish to clean by using the parchment paper), and the presentation is unusual. And to top it all it is the safest and best way to keep the nutrients. To me it's a win-win anytime, oh, and did I forget to say that kids love to help preparing the papillotes? Make it a fun activity. Once you have practiced on a few fish you can pick your favorite and match it with your favorite veggies. They are all interchangeable. *Merci*, Juliette, for introducing me to *en papillote* years ago and sharing so many recipes with me over the years. (And now they are particularly popular in France.) I think of you every time I prepare them.

COD WITH FENNEL AND ORANGE *EN PAPILLOTE*

• SERVES 4 •

4 tablespoons olive oil plus additional for parchment paper

4 (4- to 5-ounce) cod fillets

Salt and freshly ground pepper

1 fennel bulb, stalks removed, cored, and thinly sliced

1 orange, cut into 4 thick slices

1 teaspoon slightly crushed fennel seeds

2 teaspoons grated orange zest

Pinch of fleur de sel

1. Preheat the oven to 400 degrees.

2. Cut four pieces of parchment paper into 12- x 16-inch rectangles and brush the centers with olive oil. Place 1 cod fillet in the center of the parchment paper and season to taste. Top with sliced fennel and 1 slice of orange and season again. Seal the packet by bringing the sides up to the center and folding them down tightly. Seal the ends by folding each in tightly. Repeat with the remaining ingredients, creating four packets.

3. Place the packets on a baking sheet and bake for 15 to 20 minutes (the packets will be puffed and lightly browned). Remove from the oven and place one packet on each plate.

4. Meanwhile, place 4 tablespoons olive oil in a small saucepan with the fennel seeds and orange zest and warm over low heat until fragrant, about 7 minutes. Remove from the heat and pour into four small ramekins.

5. Serve each papillote accompanied by a small ramekin of olive oil and some fleur de sel.

SALMON WITH ENDIVES AND ORANGES *EN PAPILLOTE*

3 oranges

1 teaspoon olive oil plus
    additional for parchment
    paper

2 medium to large endives,
    washed and cut into thin
    strips

4 (5- to 6-ounce) salmon
    steaks

2 teaspoons peeled and
    finely grated ginger

2 teaspoons honey

Salt and freshly ground
    pepper

1. Preheat the oven to 400 degrees.

2. Remove the zest of 1 orange in long strips and julienne; reserve the orange. Place the julienned strips of orange zest in a small pot of cold water and bring to a boil. Drain the zest and set aside.

3. To prepare the orange segments, cut slices off the top and bottom of the remaining 2 oranges and then slice away the peel and pith, top to bottom, following the curve of the fruit. Working over a bowl and using a small, sharp knife, cut between the membranes to release the segments and juice of all 3 oranges.

4. Cut four pieces of parchment paper into 12- x 16-inch rectangles and brush the centers with olive oil. Place one quarter of the endive in the center of the first rectangle and top with 1 salmon steak. Add the orange segments, orange zest, ginger, and a drizzle of olive oil and honey. Season to taste and seal the packet by bringing up the sides to the center and folding them down tightly. Seal the ends by tightly folding each in. Repeat with the remaining ingredients, creating four packets.

5. Bake for 15 minutes and remove from the oven; the packets will be puffed and lightly browned. Allow to rest for 5 minutes before placing each packet on a plate and serving. Allow guests to open their packets.

SALMON WITH LEEKS AND ASPARAGUS *EN PAPILLOTE*

• SERVES 4 •

3 oranges

2 teaspoons sesame oil

2 medium carrots, peeled
   and grated

1 leek, white part only, cut
   into thin strips

8 asparagus tips, cut in half
   (reserve asparagus stalks
   for a salad)

4 (5- to 6-ounce) salmon
   steaks

Salt and freshly ground
   pepper

1 tablespoon chopped fresh
   cilantro

1 teaspoon chopped fresh
   dill

1. Preheat the oven to 400 degrees.

2. Remove the zest of 1 orange in long strips and julienne; reserve the orange. Place the julienned strips of orange zest in a small pot of cold water and bring to a boil. Drain the zest and set aside.

3. Prepare the orange segments: cut slices off the top and bottom of the remaining 2 oranges and then slice away the peel and pith, top to bottom, following the curve of the fruit. Working over a bowl and using a small, sharp knife, cut between the membranes to release the segments and juice of all 3 oranges.

4. Cut four pieces of parchment paper into 12- x 16-inch rectangles and brush the centers with sesame oil. Place one quarter of the carrots, leeks, and asparagus tips in the center of the first piece of parchment paper and top with 1 salmon steak. Add the orange segments, blanched orange zest, ¼ teaspoon sesame oil, and 1 teaspoon orange

juice. Season to taste and seal the packet by bringing up the sides to the center and folding them down tightly. Seal the ends by folding each in tightly. Repeat with the remaining ingredients, creating four packets.

5. Place the packets on a baking sheet and cook in the oven for 18 to 20 minutes. Remove from the oven (the packets will be puffed and lightly browned) and allow to rest for 5 minutes before placing each packet on a plate and serving. Allow guests to open their packets and garnish with cilantro and dill.

SEA BASS WITH SWEET SPICES
EN PAPILLOTE

1 tablespoon olive oil plus additional for parchment paper

2 yellow peppers, rinsed, seeded, and sliced lengthwise

2 medium zucchini, rinsed and cut into matchsticks

2 star anise

Pinch each of ground ginger, cinnamon, and paprika

Salt and freshly ground pepper

3 tablespoons balsamic vinegar

4 (4-ounce) sea bass fillets

2 tablespoons chopped fresh cilantro

1. Preheat the oven to 400 degrees.

2. Heat 1 tablespoon olive oil in a large skillet over medium heat. Add the yellow peppers, zucchini, star anise, and spices and sauté until the vegetables are crisp-tender, about 5 minutes. Season to taste and transfer the vegetables to a plate, removing the star anise. Deglaze the pan with the balsamic vinegar and 2 tablespoons water over medium heat, allowing the liquid to simmer for 1 to 2 minutes and reduce slightly.

3. Cut four pieces of parchment paper into 12- x 16-inch rectangles, brush the centers with olive oil, and place one quarter of the vegetables in the center of the parchment paper. Top with 1 fillet, season, drizzle with a bit of the deglazing liquid, and sprinkle with ½ tablespoon chopped cilantro. Seal the packet by bringing the sides up to the center and folding them down tightly. Seal the ends by folding each in tightly. Repeat with the remaining ingredients, creating four packets.

4. Place the papillotes on a baking sheet and bake for 15 minutes. Serve immediately.

Veggies on the Side
or in the Middle

As for veggies, these recipes evolved from experimenting with young friends and guests who have traveled and like to play with curry, capers, confit, and more.

VEGETABLE CURRY

• SERVES 4 TO 6 •

2 tablespoons olive oil

1 tablespoon unsalted butter

1 medium red onion, peeled and finely chopped

1 zucchini, washed and chopped into ½-inch cubes

1 eggplant, washed and chopped into ½-inch cubes

4 medium potatoes, peeled and chopped into ½-inch cubes

1 tablespoon curry powder

1 cinnamon stick

Salt and freshly ground pepper

2 cups water or chicken broth

1. In a large sauté pan, heat the olive oil and butter over medium-high heat. Add the onion and cook until softened, about 4 minutes. Add the zucchini, eggplant, and potatoes and mix well. Add the curry and cinnamon stick and season to taste.

2. Add the water or chicken broth, cover, and cook over low heat for 20 minutes. Remove the cover, increase the heat to medium, and cook for an additional 10 minutes, allowing the cooking liquid to thicken slightly. Season to taste and serve warm or cold.

ROASTED VEGETABLES
WITH CUMIN

4 turnips, peeled and cut
  into quarters

4 carrots, peeled and sliced
  on the bias

4 onions, peeled and sliced
  into ½-inch wedges

2 fennel bulbs, stalks and
  core discarded, cut into
  ½-inch wedges

3 tablespoons olive oil

1 teaspoon cumin seeds

Salt and freshly ground
  pepper

1. Preheat the oven to 425 degrees.

2. Place the turnips, carrots, onions, and fennel in a large bowl. Add the olive oil and cumin seeds and toss to coat.

3. Arrange the vegetables in a single layer on a baking sheet and season generously. Place in the oven and roast for 30 to 40 minutes, turning the vegetables occasionally, until they are tender and caramelized.

4. Remove from the oven and serve warm or at room temperature.

PUMPKIN AND APPLE GRATIN

2 tablespoons unsalted
  butter plus additional for
  baking dish

2 pounds pumpkin, peeled,
  seeded, and cut into
  2-inch pieces

3 baking apples (such as
  Cortland), peeled, cored
  and cut into wedges

1 tablespoon lemon juice

Salt and freshly ground
  pepper

¾ cup crème fraîche

Pinch of cinnamon

1 medium onion, peeled and
  finely chopped

5 ounces pancetta, thinly
  sliced into strips

1 tablespoon chopped
  walnuts

¾ cup feta cheese, crumbled

1 teaspoon fresh thyme

1. Preheat the oven to 350 degrees.

2. Butter a 9- x 13-inch baking dish and add the sliced pumpkin and apples. Sprinkle with lemon juice, dot with 1 tablespoon butter, and season to taste. Place in the oven and bake for 20 minutes.

3. Meanwhile, in a medium bowl combine the crème fraîche and cinnamon and set aside. Melt the remaining tablespoon of butter in a nonstick pan over medium heat and add the onion and pancetta. Sauté until the onion is softened and the pancetta has browned a bit, about 3 minutes. Remove from the heat and stir in the walnuts, feta, and thyme. Add the onion-pancetta mixture to the crème fraîche and stir to combine. Pour over the pumpkin and apples and return to the oven.

4. Continue cooking until the vegetables are tender and the top is golden, 20 to 30 minutes. Remove from the oven and serve immediately.

NOTE: *If pumpkin is not available, butternut squash makes a fine substitution.*

POÊLÉE PROVENÇALE

· SERVES 4 ·

2 tablespoons olive oil

2 zucchini, washed and
  sliced into ¼-inch-thick
  rounds

2 garlic cloves, peeled and
  minced

1 teaspoon minced fresh
  thyme

3 peppers (yellow, red, and
  orange), washed,
  seeded, and cut into thin
  strips

Salt and freshly ground
  pepper

Warm the olive oil in a large sauté pan over medium-high heat. Add the zucchini and cook, stirring, for 6 minutes. Add the garlic, thyme, and peppers and continue cooking until fragrant and the peppers are crisp-tender, about 3 minutes. Season to taste and serve warm or cold.

CARAMELIZED ENDIVES

• SERVES 4 •

1 tablespoon unsalted butter

1 tablespoon olive oil

4 endives, rinsed and
    quartered lengthwise

⅓ cup walnuts, coarsely
    chopped

1 heaping teaspoon sugar

Salt and freshly ground
    pepper

1. Heat the butter and olive oil in a large sauté pan over medium-high heat. Add the endives and cook, stirring, until golden, about 5 minutes.

2. Add the walnuts and sugar and continue cooking, gently stirring, until caramelized, about 3 more minutes. Remove from the heat, season to taste, and serve.

ROASTED CAULIFLOWER WITH RAISINS AND CAPERS

• SERVES 4 •

⅓ cup golden raisins

2 tablespoons red wine vinegar

1 large head cauliflower, trimmed and cut into small florets

5 tablespoons olive oil

Salt and freshly ground pepper

1 tablespoon capers, drained and chopped

3 tablespoons pine nuts

1 tablespoon finely chopped fresh parsley

1. Preheat the oven to 400 degrees.

2. Combine the raisins and vinegar in a small bowl and allow the raisins to "plump" for about 30 minutes.

3. Place the cauliflower florets on a baking sheet and drizzle with 2 tablespoons olive oil. Season to taste and roast in the oven for 25 minutes, turning occasionally.

4. In a medium bowl, combine the raisins and any remaining vinegar, capers, pine nuts, parsley, and the remaining 3 tablespoons olive oil. Season to taste.

5. Remove the baking sheet from the oven and pour the raisin-caper mixture over the cauliflower, tossing gently. Return the baking sheet to the oven and continue roasting for an additional 15 minutes or until the cauliflower is tender and caramelized. Remove from the oven, place in a bowl, and season to taste. Serve warm or at room temperature.

EGGPLANT WITH CURRY AND HONEY

2 large shallots, peeled and minced

1 lemon confit, drained and diced

4 teaspoons honey

Juice of 1 lemon

4 tablespoons olive oil

1 teaspoon curry powder

4 medium eggplants, rinsed and quartered lengthwise

Salt and freshly ground pepper

1. Preheat the oven to 375 degrees.

2. In a medium bowl, combine the shallots, lemon confit, honey, lemon juice, olive oil, and curry.

3. Place the eggplants on a baking sheet in a single layer. Season to taste and pour the lemon-curry-honey mixture over the eggplant, tossing gently to coat evenly.

4. Bake for 10 minutes, lower the temperature to 300 degrees, and baste with the lemon-curry-honey mixture. Continue cooking for 1 hour or until the eggplant is slightly caramelized and soft, turning occasionally.

ENDIVES *CONFITES* WITH BLUE CHEESE CROSTINI

• SERVES 4 •

6 tablespoons butter

4 medium to large endives,
 rinsed and cut lengthwise
 into thin strips

2 tablespoons honey

½ cup whole milk

Fresh thyme to taste

Fleur de sel and freshly
 ground pepper

4 slices whole wheat bread,
 toasted

6 ounces blue cheese, at
 room temperature

1. In a large skillet, melt the butter over medium-low heat. Add the endives, honey, milk, and thyme. Bring to a simmer, reduce the heat, cover, and cook until the endives are tender, about 30 minutes.

2. To serve, season the endives with fleur de sel and pepper and serve immediately in a soup dish with a slice of toasted bread spread with blue cheese.

ONION *POÊLÉE* WITH APPLES

• SERVES 4 •

2 ounces bacon, diced

4 tablespoons unsalted
    butter

1 pound onions, peeled,
    halved, and thinly sliced

3 apples, peeled, cored, and
    sliced

Salt and freshly ground
    pepper

1. Cook the bacon in a nonstick skillet over medium heat until golden and crisp. Transfer to a paper towel–lined plate to drain.

2. Add the butter to the skillet and melt over medium heat. Add the onions and cook until softened, stirring occasionally, about 10 minutes. Add the apples and bacon and season to taste. Continue cooking for another 10 minutes, stirring occasionally and adding a bit of water if the apples and onions stick. Remove from the heat and serve immediately.

CARROT PARSNIP PURÉE

• SERVES 4 •

1 pound carrots, peeled and chopped

2 parsnips, peeled and chopped

1 medium sweet potato, peeled and chopped

3 tablespoons chilled unsalted butter

Pinch of sugar (optional)

Salt and freshly ground pepper

1 teaspoon freshly grated nutmeg

2 tablespoons crème fraîche

1. In a medium saucepan, combine the carrots, parsnips, sweet potato, 1 tablespoon butter, and a pinch of sugar, if using, and season to taste. Add ½ cup water, cover, and cook over medium-high heat for 15 minutes. Uncover and cook for an additional 10 minutes or until the vegetables are very tender and the cooking liquid has reduced and become syrupy.

2. Remove the saucepan from the heat and carefully transfer the vegetables to a blender. Add the remaining 2 tablespoons butter, nutmeg, and crème fraîche and purée until smooth. Season to taste and serve immediately.

LENTIL, FENNEL, AND ORANGE SALAD

4 cups water or vegetable broth

1 cup lentils

2 oranges

2 tablespoons red wine or sherry vinegar

½ medium shallot, minced (about 1 tablespoon)

1 teaspoon peeled and finely grated fresh ginger

4 tablespoons olive oil

1 fennel bulb, washed, trimmed, quartered lengthwise, and thinly sliced crosswise

Salt and freshly ground pepper

1. Bring the water or vegetable broth and lentils to a boil in a large saucepan. Reduce the heat and simmer, uncovered, until the lentils are just tender, about 20 minutes. Drain and reserve.

2. To prepare the orange segments, cut slices off the top and bottom of the oranges and then slice away the peel and pith from the oranges, following the curve of the fruit. Working over a bowl and using a small sharp knife, cut between the membranes to release the segments and juice.

3. In a separate small bowl, whisk together the vinegar, shallot, ginger, and olive oil. In a large bowl, combine the lentils, fennel, and orange segments and juice. Add the vinaigrette and mix well. Taste, correct the seasoning, and serve.

LEEK AND ZUCCHINI SALAD

• SERVES 4 •

8 medium leeks, white parts
 only, quartered and
 rinsed in cold water to
 remove any grit

4 small zucchini, cut
 crosswise into 2-inch
 pieces and quartered

1 teaspoon Dijon mustard

1 teaspoon acacia honey

2 tablespoons lemon juice

2 tablespoons olive oil

Salt and freshly ground
 pepper

2 tablespoons chopped fresh
 dill

1. Bring a pot of salted water to a boil over medium-high heat. Add the leeks and cook for 7 minutes. Add the zucchini and cook until crisp-tender, about 2 minutes. Drain and let cool.

2. In a medium bowl, whisk together the mustard, honey, lemon juice, and olive oil. Season to taste. Add the leeks and zucchini and toss gently to combine.

3. Serve garnished with dill.

SWEET-AND-SOUR
CARROT SALAD

Juice of 1 orange

Juice of ½ lemon

Pinch of cinnamon

1 teaspoon honey

3 tablespoons olive oil

Salt and freshly ground
   pepper

1 pound carrots, washed and
   grated

1 apple, peeled and grated

⅓ cup walnuts

1. Mix the orange and lemon juices, add the cinnamon and honey, and slowly drizzle in the olive oil, whisking to combine. Season to taste.

2. Place the grated carrots, apple, and walnuts in a large salad bowl. Add the dressing, toss gently to combine, and serve.

Chapter Five

CLOSURES—SWEET, CHOCOLATE, AND OTHERWISE

I love sweets. Did I need to say that? Growing up with a mother, grandmother, aunt, and many relatives who loved baking, the sweet smell and taste of something in the oven invaded my childhood. Desserts and things sweet are mildly addictive—the more you get, it seems, the more you need to feel fully satisfied. Okay, for some of us sweets are fully addictive. It took my year in Weston, Massachusetts, and gaining too many kilos, to later understand the power of sugar and its control of our brain. But to borrow from *Alice*, "The question is," said Humpty Dumpty, "which is to be master— that's all."

For me a little something sweet at the end of a meal, even one bite of chocolate, clicks shut the lunch pail oh so perfectly, achieving a balanced closure. I should emphasize, a *little* some-

thing at the end of the meal (remember portion proportions), and also that perfectly ripe fruit in season is nature's best way to round out a healthy and satisfying meal. Sweet, fresh fruit—berries or globes of fruit—is not an acquired taste. When they are ripe and sweet, people adore them. They are an acquired habit, however. One that advertisers of gooey desserts have defended against. A fresh peach or slice of melon or a cupcake?

If you are looking to ban a few food offenders, I implore you to reconsider, for one illustrative seductress, the cupcake. I know: I am asking for a lot. It is covered with a lot of childhood memories. But the reality of most cupcakes' unnecessary and excessive sweetness was brought home to me twice in the past year. (I am citing the cupcake, but you can come up with apt alternatives that will bring the eat-with-your-head-as-well-as-your-senses point home.)

There's a bakery in our Greenwich Village neighborhood in New York City that was made famous via the *Sex and the City* TV series. The series may be no more—though everywhere around the world in reruns—but the bakery is very much alive in the present with hordes of people lining up to buy its cupcakes. It is a quaint little bakery on a charming tree-lined street, and it is nothing to see twenty or thirty people on line stretching around the corner to gain access to the privilege of purchasing one of these coveted treats. What is their magic? My husband grew up on cupcakes, so once I bought him one of this store's famous "cakes" for his birthday. Surprise: he couldn't finish it and did not enjoy it. He said it was so sweet it was what we call *écœurant* (the extreme opposite of appetizing).

The second surprise came when I was passing by the shop early in the morning (before the lines) with a young foreign friend who wanted to take a picture of it. We talked with one of the staff to ask about the icing and coloring and he said, "You don't want to know or you wouldn't touch the stuff." We explained that we had no intention of buying, even less eating them, but were just taking pictures for a New York photo album. Then he added, "The icing is bad enough, but the inside is just as bad." (Now how's that for a loyal and helpful employee? Or should I say former employee . . .)

The store is such a curiosity that I've also watched on many occasions, particularly on weekend afternoons, people emerging victorious after their twenty minutes on line with a cupcake or more and then devouring it in under two minutes (more like one minute) flat out right there on the street outside the shop. Forget the pleasure factor; that's not savoring or experiencing pleasure. That's a quick fix. And what does that do to your body? I suspect you'll be craving sweets for days. It surely sends the wrong message to your brain, and yet so many of us wonder about our cravings. Enough studies have proved that sugary treats trigger mood swings tied to our soaring blood sugar levels and prime us for energy crashes followed by more cravings for sweets. What a vicious circle. Sweets are tough to walk away from, so it's up to you to come up with the tricks that work for you: don't walk by the pastry shops (that's one of mine), don't bring home more than a reasonable portion of dessert or you'll eat the whole thing, avoid strange encounters of the sugary kind at work—walk away.

Enough. This chapter is a celebration of desserts and the pleasures they bring (really) and not a discourse on their evil ways. One of the things I have been implicitly highlighting, and now explicitly, is that desserts and other sweets should not exist often in isolation. Okay, an ice cream cone now and again is a pleasure not a crime. At the end of a meal laden with protein and varied food groups, a dessert is a perfect and healthy closure. Enjoy it. Just remember portion size and balance over a few days.

Prufrock may have "known them all already, known them all:—/have known the evenings, mornings, afternoons,/. . . have measured out my life with coffee spoons . . ." Well, I have tasted them all, eaten them all. I have measured out my life with chocolate mousse, apricot tart, cannelé, tiramisù, crème brûlée, éclair, blueberry tart, opéra, mille-feuille. No regrets. My weight is still normal. (I should have mentioned coffee ice cream.)

Here then for your pleasure, I offer desserts that are mostly made with fresh fruits plus the occasional tart or cake and, *bien sûr*, a little chocolate that will satisfy you with a mini portion. Enjoy.

APPLE COMPOTE
WITH PISTACHIOS

4 *Golden Delicious apples,*
  peeled, cored, and cut
  into small dice

1 *tablespoon lemon juice*

2 *tablespoons unsalted*
  butter

3 *tablespoons sugar*

1 *cinnamon stick*

2 *tablespoons pistachio nuts,*
  chopped

1. Combine the apples and lemon juice.

2. Melt the butter in a medium sauté pan over medium-low heat. Add the apples, sugar, and cinnamon stick and cook for 20 minutes, stirring occasionally. Add the pistachios and cook for an additional 10 minutes. Remove the apple compote from the pan and serve at room temperature, garnished with the cinnamon stick.

PEAR AND DATE AU GRATIN

• SERVES 4 •

3 ripe Comice pears, peeled, cored, and thinly sliced

8 dates, julienned

4 egg yolks

⅛ teaspoon wasabi (this Japanese horseradish adds a touch of spicy heat and flavor)

½ cup crème fraîche

1. Preheat the broiler or set the oven to 400 degrees and grease four individual ramekins with butter.

2. Divide the sliced pears and dates equally among four ramekins.

3. In a stand mixer and using a whisk attachment, mix together the egg yolks and wasabi. Add the crème fraîche and mix until combined.

4. Pour the crème fraîche mixture over the fruit and place under the broiler for 4 minutes (or place in the oven for 8 minutes). Remove from the oven and serve warm.

FRUIT SALAD WITH QUINOA

· SERVES 4 TO 6 ·

1 cup quinoa

½ cup freshly squeezed
  grapefruit juice

3 tablespoons honey

½ teaspoon lime zest

1 pound mixed fruit (such
  as strawberries, grapes,
  melon, blueberries, and
  raspberries)

Fresh mint sprigs

1. Cook the quinoa according to the package instructions. Drain and cool.

2. In a small bowl, whisk together the grapefruit juice, honey, and lime zest. Set aside.

3. Prepare the fruit: slice the strawberries and grapes in half; peel and dice the melon. Place all the fruit in a serving bowl and add the cooled quinoa. Add the grapefruit juice mixture and toss gently to combine. Garnish with mint and serve.

Smoothies and Verrines

Verrines are those small, clear glass containers—some only a bit taller and a bit bigger than shot glasses and other glass sizes—the French have fallen in love with to serve savory or sweet food. Go to one of those grand three Michelin–star restaurants and wannabes and the pricey menus include additional free goodies, often including one, two, or three miniature verrines as preappetizers and also sometimes as predesserts. It has been an increasing trend for at least a decade. Nowadays, home cooks are getting the hang of serving an appetite opener or modest tasting in a glass as they have been featured in magazines, pastry shops, television cooking programs, and small cookbooks dedicated exclusively to the art of the verrine.

To me, their first and best appeal is visual. The layers (often three), colors, textures, and top garnish make them look like a small piece of art, and three in a row on an oblong dish can easily look like a miniature painting that you can actually eat. I've been serving them for years, especially in the summer in Provence and the "wow" sign is a given when they appear on the breakfast table, a buffet, a party, or a sit-down meal. Bringing the same food in a bowl or dish just does not create that surprise.

The concept is also a practical one (no doubt a reason French women love it) as verrines can be prepared in advance, eaten anywhere from a terrace (yours or a café), a bench in a park, a picnic, or any party where people can move around eating or drinking. And the portions are small: It really is all in the three bites, *n'est-ce pas?*

Smoothies—a big, very big, cousin of sorts (a few times removed) of verrines—gained popularity in America first before becoming globalized (no doubt every culture will have some claim on their origin; blended fruits and vegetables are hardly new, but the widespread availability of electric blenders is). The best are those freshly made and consumed before the vitamins and other elements start to degrade. Beware of those in supermarkets, where additional sugars of the strange kind are added. And beware of preservatives and artificial ingredients in the processed variety.

RED BERRY SMOOTHIE

• SERVES 2 •

1 cup fresh strawberries,
    rinsed and hulled

1 cup frozen raspberries

⅔ cup plain Greek-style
    yogurt

½ cup apple juice

Place all the ingredients in a blender and purée until smooth. Serve at once.

RASPBERRY-BANANA SMOOTHIE

• SERVES 2 •

⅔ cup plain Greek-style
   yogurt

½ cup 2% milk

1 cup frozen raspberries

1 ripe banana, peeled and
   sliced

Place all the ingredients in a blender and purée until smooth. Serve at once.

RHUBARB SMOOTHIE

• SERVES 2 •

....

½ pound rhubarb, cut into
  small pieces
1 teaspoon honey
Zest and juice of 1 orange
1 banana, peeled and sliced
2 to 4 fresh or frozen
  strawberries

1. In a small saucepan, combine the rhubarb, honey, and orange zest. Add ¼ cup water, cover, and cook over low heat until the rhubarb is very tender, about 20 minutes.

2. Remove the saucepan from the heat and cool (this may be done in advance).

3. Place the rhubarb in a blender with the orange juice, banana, and strawberries and purée. Serve immediately.

RASPBERRY-BLACKBERRY RICE
PUDDING VERRINES

• SERVES 6 TO 8 •

....

*5 ounces raspberries, rinsed
  and patted dry with
  paper towels*

*5 ounces blackberries, rinsed
  and patted dry with
  paper towels*

5 ounces sugar

9 ounces short-grain rice

2 quarts milk, whole or 2%

*1 teaspoon pure vanilla
  extract*

4 egg yolks

2 ounces butter

*5 ounces strawberries,
  rinsed, patted dry with
  paper towels, and cut
  into halves*

Fresh mint sprigs

1. Put the raspberries and blackberries in a salad bowl and cover with 1 ounce of sugar. Reserve in the refrigerator.

2. Bring 1½ quarts of water to a boil. Add the rice and cook for 2 minutes in boiling water. Drain and reserve.

3. Bring the milk to a boil in a heavy saucepan. Add the rice, the remaining 4 ounces sugar, and the vanilla. Cook over low heat for 30 minutes and stir gently a couple of times. It is important to watch this process so that the rice does not get gluey. Off the heat, add the egg yolks one at a time, add the butter, and over low heat combine and cook for 1 minute. Let the mixture cool.

4. Add 2 tablespoons water to the raspberry-blackberry mixture and put through a sieve to obtain a coulis. Cover the bottom of the verrines with the coulis. Top with the rice pudding. Garnish with the strawberries and fresh mint.

PINEAPPLE, YOGURT, AND CHOCOLATE VERRINES

• SERVES 4 •

· ·

1 fresh pineapple

Zest and juice of 1 orange

Pinch of saffron

3½ ounces dark chocolate, chopped (70% to 80% cacao preferred)

3 tablespoons 2% milk

1 cup plain Greek-style yogurt

1 tablespoon crème fraîche

1. Peel and core the pineapple, then cut into small dice. In a medium bowl, combine the pineapple, orange zest and juice, and saffron. Reserve.

2. Place the chocolate in a bowl. Pour the milk into a small saucepan and bring to a simmer. Remove from the heat, pour the milk over the chocolate, and let stand for 2 minutes before stirring the chocolate until smooth. Allow the chocolate to cool until just warm to the touch.

3. When the chocolate has cooled, add the yogurt, crème fraîche, and 1 to 2 tablespoons of juice from the chopped pineapple and stir until combined. Refrigerate for at least 15 minutes and up to 6 hours.

4. To serve, alternate layers of pineapple with a small amount of juice and the chocolate-yogurt mixture in individual serving bowls or small glasses. Serve at once.

CHOCOLATE-COFFEE VERRINES

• SERVES 6 TO 8 •

FOR THE COFFEE MOUSSE

4 egg whites

Pinch of salt

3 tablespoons strong espresso

5 ounces sugar

FOR THE CHOCOLATE MOUSSE

12 ounces dark chocolate (70% to 80% cacao preferred)

4 ounces butter, at room temperature

2 egg yolks

5 egg whites

1½ ounces sugar

FOR THE GARNISH

Little squares of high-quality milk chocolate

Fresh mint sprigs

TO MAKE THE COFFEE MOUSSE

1. Beat the egg whites with a pinch of salt until very firm. Add the coffee and sugar while continuing to beat. Refrigerate for 2 hours.

TO MAKE THE CHOCOLATE MOUSSE

2. Melt the chocolate over a pot of simmering water. Remove from the heat and add the butter and egg yolks, mixing gently. Beat the egg whites with the sugar into soft peaks. Incorporate a third of the chocolate-butter mixture, mix, and add the rest, mixing delicately. Refrigerate for 2 hours.

3. To serve, put a layer of coffee mousse at the bottom of each verrine, top with a layer of chocolate mousse, and decorate with a square of milk chocolate and a sprig of mint.

CRÊPES

My New England friend, Sarah, who loves things French and studied cooking in Paris, lived on crêpes when she was a student there. She continued the practice as a busy stagiaire *in restaurants in France. Now that she's back in New England, this is her basic crêpe recipe.*

1 cup flour
1¼ cups 2% or whole milk
2 eggs
2 tablespoons butter, melted
¼ teaspoon salt
Butter for pan

1. Combine the flour, milk, eggs, melted butter, and salt in a blender and mix just until combined, about 10 seconds (make sure the flour is fully incorporated).

2. Refrigerate the crêpe batter for at least 1 hour and up to 2 days before cooking.

3. Heat a small nonstick pan over medium-high heat and brush the surface with butter. Pour a small amount of batter onto the center of the pan and swirl the pan to evenly distribute in a thin layer. Cook for about 30 seconds; the top of the crêpe will appear dry and the edges will start to crisp. Loosen the edges and flip with a spatula. Cook for another 10 seconds and carefully slide the crêpe onto a plate. Repeat with the remaining batter, brushing the pan surface lightly with butter each time. Crêpes may be stacked on top of one another and kept warm. Serve immediately.

VARIATIONS

SAVORY: *Mix 2 tablespoons finely chopped chives (or another favorite herb) into the batter.*

SWEET: *Add 2 tablespoons of your favorite liqueur to the batter or 1 tablespoon citrus zest.*

For serving, try these toppings:

- *butter and sugar*

- *shaved bittersweet chocolate*

- *butter, lemon juice, sugar*

- *sliced fresh fruit and yogurt*

- *grated cheese, boiled ham*

- *Parmesan and grated apple*

MANGO LASSI, THE FRENCH WAY

• SERVES 2 •

Tusshar, my French friend's companion, likes to drink mango lassi (a South Indian drink), but he used canned mango with syrup and added sugar. Not our cup of tea, we said. We like ours thicker and less sweet, and we serve it at the end of a meal. Kids love it. So here is our Frenchie version.

1 mango, peeled and diced (about ¾ cup)

1 cup fromage blanc (or buttermilk)

1 cup water

2 teaspoons honey

Pinch of salt

Combine the mango with the *fromage blanc*, water, honey, and salt in a blender and purée at medium speed until smooth. Serve immediately.

YOGURT AND NUT "COCKTAIL"

• SERVES 2 •

1½ cups plain Greek-style yogurt

2 tablespoons chopped almonds

2 tablespoons pine nuts

2 ice cubes

1 teaspoon cinnamon

3 teaspoons honey

1. Place half of the yogurt along with the almonds, pine nuts, and ice cubes in a blender and purée until smooth.

2. Add the remaining yogurt, cinnamon, and honey and blend again until smooth and frothy. Serve at once.

YOGURT AND FRUIT SALAD

• SERVES 4 •

1 pear, peeled, cored, and
   diced

2 kiwi, peeled and sliced

2 peaches, rinsed and cut
   into small dice

2 tablespoons sugar

¼ cup pistachio nuts,
   coarsely chopped

1 banana, peeled and thinly
   sliced

2 cups plain goat milk
   yogurt (or cow's milk
   yogurt)

2 teaspoons strawberry or
   raspberry jam

1. Place the pear, kiwi, and peaches in a bowl and sprinkle with 1 tablespoon sugar. Mix gently, cover with plastic wrap, and refrigerate for 30 minutes.

2. Mix the remaining tablespoon of sugar with the pistachios and set aside.

3. To serve, add the banana slices to the fruit salad and gently toss. Divide the fruit salad among four clear glass bowls. Top with a layer of yogurt and sprinkle with pistachios. Garnish with a dollop of jam and serve.

YOGURT AND OATMEAL CAKE

• MAKES ONE 9- X 13-INCH CAKE •

1 cup boiling water

1 cup old-fashioned oatmeal

Butter, softened for baking dish

¾ cup brown sugar

¾ cup granulated sugar

8 tablespoons (1 stick) unsalted butter, melted

2 eggs

⅔ cup plain yogurt

1 teaspoon pure vanilla extract

1½ cups unbleached white flour

1 teaspoon baking powder

1 teaspoon baking soda

½ teaspoon salt

1 teaspoon cinnamon

½ teaspoon ground allspice

¼ teaspoon freshly grated nutmeg

1 teaspoon orange zest

Coffee ice cream (optional)

1. Pour the boiling water over the rolled oats and let stand for 15 minutes.

2. Preheat the oven to 350 degrees. Butter a 9- x 13-inch baking dish and set aside.

3. In a large bowl, mix together the sugars and melted butter. Add the eggs and whisk until well blended. Stir in the yogurt and vanilla and set aside.

4. In a separate bowl, combine the flour, baking powder, baking soda, salt, and spices. Add half of the flour mixture and the oats to the wet ingredients and stir until blended. Add the remaining flour mixture and orange zest and mix gently until combined. Pour the batter into the baking dish and bake for 25 minutes or until a knife inserted all the way comes out clean. Remove from the oven and cool before cutting and serving. Serve with a scoop of coffee ice cream, if desired.

PANNA COTTA

• SERVES 8 •

....

My Tuscan friend, Emiliana, first introduced me to this molded chilled dessert ages ago in a small, unpretentious restaurant in Forte dei Marmi, near Lucca. It was love at first sight and taste, and I'd never reveal how many times I've made panna cotta for added culinary entertainment. Guests often think it takes a great dessert maker to produce this—not at all. It's about the easiest, fastest dessert that has chutzpah, and it's impossible to blow it. I tell them so, but no one believes me. Try it.

1 tablespoon unflavored gelatin

2 tablespoons cold water

1 cup 2% or whole milk

2 cups heavy cream

¼ cup sugar

1½ teaspoons pure vanilla extract

1. In a small saucepan, sprinkle the gelatin over the water and let soften for about 1 minute. Heat the mixture over low heat until the gelatin is dissolved. Remove from the heat.

2. In a large saucepan, bring the milk, cream, and sugar just to a boil over moderately high heat, stirring once in a while. Remove the pan from the heat and whisk in the gelatin mixture and vanilla. Divide the mixture among eight ½-cup ramekins and cool to room temperature.

3. Cover with plastic film and chill for 4 hours or overnight.

4. To unmold, just before serving, dip the ramekins one at a time in a bowl of hot water for a few seconds. Run a thin knife around the edge of each ramekin and invert on the center of a dessert plate.

NOTE: *Serve with fresh mixed berries (strawberries and blackberries or raspberries and blueberries) in the summer, an apple-pear compote or cranberry chutney in the winter, or make a fruit coulis with a mango. The choice of accompaniment is infinite. Place a mint or basil leaf in the middle of the panna cotta (this adds a nice colorful touch).*

LEMON CURD

• SERVES 2 TO 4 •

After tomatoes and strawberries, lemon is probably my favorite fruit (today at least, but cherries or apricots don't count as their season is, alas, so short). I use lemon with abandon for my magical breakfast but also with fish, veggies, salads, and in citron pressé *as a thirst quencher. Then, there are desserts, and a French lemon tart (oh so tart and tangy) is one of my favorite things. You can keep the meringue. Here is a curd I often make and use to make* tartines *for visiting kids or to make a last-minute tart and garnish a* pâte brisée *mold or make small individual tarts. Of course, you can also use the curd in a* verrine *with a dollop of cream and store-bought tuile cookies.*

⅔ cup lemon juice (about 3 lemons, preferably organic)

2 teaspoons lemon zest

6 egg yolks

5 ounces sugar

¾ teaspoon butter

1. In a stainless-steel bowl over simmering water, combine the lemon juice, lemon zest, egg yolks, and sugar and whisk continuously until the mixture is smooth and has thickened to the consistency of sour cream, 8 to 10 minutes.

2. Remove the bowl from over the water, add the butter and continue whisking until smooth and the curd has cooled a bit. Cover with plastic wrap and refrigerate for 24 hours.

NOTE: *Curd will keep for 1 week, chilled and covered. Since it's addictive, you may want to double the recipe next time you make it. Save and use the egg whites for omelets or frittatas.*

(EGGLESS) CHOCOLATE MOUSSE WITH CARDAMOM

6 cardamom pods, slightly crushed

2 cups heavy cream

5 ounces dark chocolate (70 to 80% cacao preferred), chopped

1 tablespoon pistachio nuts, shelled and toasted

1. Place the cardamom and ½ cup heavy cream in a small, heavy saucepan and bring to a boil. Meanwhile, place the chopped chocolate in a large bowl. Remove the saucepan from the heat and pour the cream through a fine-mesh sieve over the chopped chocolate. Allow the chocolate to melt for 2 minutes, then stir until smooth; cool until the chocolate-cream mixture is just warm to the touch.

2. Whip the remaining 1½ cups chilled heavy cream until stiff peaks form (be careful not to overwhip). Gently fold half of the whipped cream into the chocolate mixture to lighten and then incorporate the remaining whipped cream; the mousse will be a bit soft. Spoon the mousse into serving dishes, cover, and refrigerate for at least 2 hours. Before serving, garnish with pistachio nuts.

MADELEINES AU CHOCOLAT

• MAKES ABOUT 20 MADELEINES •

Madeleines, those cookie-size, shell-shape cakes, may make you reread Proust's Re-membrance of Things Past (although dunking madeleines in tea is not my way of enjoying them, stale or not). My childhood memories are filled with eating freshly made madeleines by Mamie. *None of my girlfriends' mothers ever made them since the local pâtisserie carried them. Apparently,* Mamie*'s versions were better or shall we say different, freshly made and eaten only when warm. Usually, she made standard madeleines, although once in a while she would surprise us with our favorite,* les madeleines au chocolat. *The ritual was always the same: They were served for the* goûter, *afternoon snack after school, and I could bring a friend. In the spring, we would go outside and eat them at the garden table, and in wintertime, in our large kitchen, at the table, sometimes with hot chocolate. Just as Proust's madeleine started his journey of recollection, these "cookie-cakes" always remind me of a story from my own childhood (which my family referred to as* de la souris et des madeleines*).*

When I went to primary school (age six) I made a new friend, Danielle, whom I invited home on a cold, snowy December day. Mamie *was working in the front of the house and announced that the madeleines were just out of the oven and cooling off in the kitchen. By then, I knew what to do (I never waited until they were at room tem-perature as I liked them best a touch warm). That day, however, as we entered the kitchen we spotted a mouse on the floor near the work area where the madeleines were resting. We were both equally scared of mice and jumped on the kitchen table speech-less and paralyzed. Time passed, not a word was spoken, and neither of us would go down from the kitchen table while the mouse was wandering about ignoring us (fortu-nately not going near the madeleines but sniffing the aroma for sure). I don't remem-ber how long we stood on that table (I can still see myself on the table), it felt like hours, but suddenly Mother came in wondering why there was such silence, and seeing us in that position started laughing her head off. She scared away the mouse. We blushed, and that day the madeleines did not taste the same, but it was not because they were completely cold. For years, every time my mother wanted to illustrate the gourmande I was, she would tell whoever was there the story* de la souris et des madeleines. *I still love chocolate madeleines best, and I still don't care for mice in the house. And who doesn't love chocolate?*

3½ ounces dark chocolate (70% to 80% cacao preferred)

6 tablespoons unsalted butter, cut into small pieces

½ cup plus 3 tablespoons all-purpose flour

1 teaspoon baking powder

2 large eggs

½ cup sugar

1. Combine the chocolate and butter in a bowl set over a pot of simmering water and melt, stirring until smooth. Remove the bowl from the heat and let cool.

2. In a small bowl, sift together the flour and baking powder and reserve.

3. In a stand mixer, whisk the eggs until frothy. Gradually add the sugar and continue whisking until the mixture is pale yellow and has thickened, 2 to 3 minutes. Add the cooled chocolate-butter mixture, folding it in gently until well combined. Carefully fold in the flour mixture and mix just until combined. Cover the batter and refrigerate for 3 hours.

4. Preheat the oven to 400 degrees. Spoon the chilled batter in (preferably) nonstick madeleine molds, filling them three quarters full. Bake for 11 to 13 minutes until they are puffed and spring back to the touch. Do not overbake. Remove from the oven and unmold directly onto a cooling rack. Serve slightly warm or at room temperature. Madeleines can be kept for 2 to 3 days in an airtight container.

SPICED CHOCOLATE MOUSSE

• SERVES 4 •

· ·

7 ounces dark chocolate (70 to 80% cacao preferred), chopped

4 eggs, separated, at room temperature

⅓ cup plus 2 tablespoons sugar

½ cup crème fraîche

Zest of 1 orange

Zest of 1 lemon

Pinch of cinnamon

Pinch of freshly grated nutmeg

1 teaspoon pure vanilla extract

1. In a double boiler insert set over barely simmering water, melt the chocolate, stirring until smooth. Remove from the heat and let the chocolate cool slightly. It should feel warm but not hot to the touch.

2. Meanwhile, place the egg whites and a pinch of sugar in the bowl of a stand mixer and whisk for 2 to 3 minutes on medium-high speed while gradually incorporating half of the sugar. When the egg whites almost form stiff peaks, add the remaining sugar and beat until glossy. Remove the whipped egg whites and place in a large bowl. Clean the mixing bowl and add the crème fraîche, citrus zests, cinnamon, nutmeg, vanilla, and egg yolks and mix for 20 seconds on medium-high speed. Add the warm chocolate and beat until smooth.

3. Carefully fold the chocolate mixture into the egg whites and gently mix. Serve, garnished with additional crème fraîche and orange zest, if desired, or refrigerate, covered, until ready to serve. This may be made one day in advance (let stand at room temperature for 20 minutes before serving if chilled).

Chapter Six

PUTTING IT
ALL TOGETHER

I love the phrase "putting it all together." It implies a little mental and manual dexterity, and in a world where so many things take so long to come together (ever move to a new house or apartment? Or renovate a kitchen or bath? Or write a marketing plan?) that they bring discomfort not comfort, open-endedness not closure.

Planning and making a dish and planning a menu can be highly satisfying activities. Almost instant gratification. (Note I did not include cleaning up afterward.) I used to go to the office day after day and plug away on this campaign or that challenge only to return the next day and the next to continue the task. Cooking, however, is where you can get your hands dirty and in short order eat your efforts. That's satisfaction. What's not great and healthy about that?

As a CEO I used knowledge and experience more than intellect. Perhaps intellect got me where I landed, but my value to my company was that I knew what to do immediately in a host of challenging situations. I knew how to read the tea leaves and react favorably. There is no substitute for experience or a knowledge base learned by fire. But I did not use the same brain cells that I did the first time I read Pascal. Sure, I gained satisfaction when I was part of a solution or part of a winning action, but mostly these played out over time, often months, regularly a year or more. In the kitchen, I had and have to plan, organize, and then juggle three things at once, be ready to adjust on the fly, and use brain cells—I would say intellect and focus—as challenging in the moment as I found in a corner office. And the reward—almost immediate. What a healthy sense of achievement when the dish comes out of the oven or is plated appealingly for dinner. Cooking is a form of mental health—at least for me.

And that's why I like "putting it all together." Besides, it is the title of a musical revue of Stephen Sondheim music that plays in my head when I say the phrase.

What follows are some basic menus and some not so basic entertainment menus. Think of them as a starting point, a stimulation point, perhaps a launching point. I like to read recipes, menus, and watch cooking shows. I almost never reproduce what I mentally ingest. But they are warm-ups for me and stimulate me to imagine what I would and indeed do in the kitchen. Perhaps what follows will do the same for you. But they might also help you break old habits and reinvent what you eat—to try something new and to learn a new song. Sometimes we all need a little easy follow-along guidance to move on down the road.

Here are a few more divergent thoughts on menus, consumption, and balance. First is to remember the phrase "exceptions prove the rule." I believe in a three meals a day rule, with the following exception. Sometimes, two will have to do. That happens, say, when you are traveling in different time zones. Or you sleep exceedingly late on vacation, in another time zone or not, then brunch is the order of the day. Remember to balance your intake over time so you don't run down or overeat later. When you are down to two meals, add some protein such as eggs, ham, or even some smoked salmon to your initial meal. Then to pace your body and energy level, you'll need some sort of "snack" before dinner (three meals), even just a few nuts (and I really mean a few as in three to five); for me, a good choice is always a mix of plain yogurt with fruit.

Beware of too much raw veggies at any time, particularly in the summer months. The fashion for eating raw did not last very long in the United States and for good and obvious reasons. If raw vegetables fill you up due to their water and fiber content, you'll eat less of a main course but risk getting hungry a few hours later and a call for fat or sweet stuff (read cupcake or granola bar, or fill in the blank) will be waiting for you. They also may get boring in taste and texture and chewing action, inhibiting diversity of experience and pleasure.

As for sweet stuff, the best placement is to eat dessert at the end of a meal. No news there. But why? This way they assimilate better and more slowly than if eaten by themselves in the middle of the day outside mealtimes. And with dessert you give your body its "sweet" craving dose on a semi-full stomach with *you* controlling (and capable of controlling) the portion.

In putting it all together, remember to avoid fried foods as much as possible and when included in a meal to really remember portion sizes (that small apple is a normal portion rule). You also need to be sensitive to your intake of fatty and overly salty food. Salt makes you want to eat more, which easily explains why chip addicts eat the whole bag, mostly on autopilot and not realizing that salt calls for more salt just as sugar calls for more sugar. And salt makes you thirsty and what you subsequently drink can increase your imbalances of the unhealthy kind. And if these mini reminders seem basic, I have learned from my websites and presentations, including television appearances and "makeover" spots, how often we are blind to the truth about what we're putting into our bodies. Hey, I used to put a lot of sugar in my coffee—now none.

Favor soups at lunch and dinner and at any season. They are easy and healthy additions to most menus. Many of us don't think about soup in the summertime, but almost any *soupe glacée* is delicious and our body loves their cool refreshment. In my case, whatever is left in my veggie bin—a few peppers, tomatoes, cucumber, whatever—is rinsed, roughly chopped, and with herbs, spices, water added, plus a few minutes in the blender, ready to be served with a drizzle of olive oil, fresh herbs, and a slice of whole wheat or any good bread.

For those who enjoy and are able to eat seafood, there are lots of healthy and pleasure bonuses, and as they are not readily gulped down fast, they force well-paced ingestion. Even peeling your shrimp or cleaning your lobster takes time. Remember it takes 20 minutes for the satiety signal to kick in, so don't rush your meal or you may well overeat. Sit down, chew, and savor; all are necessary for assimilation and digestion. And you'll keep a flat stomach, too.

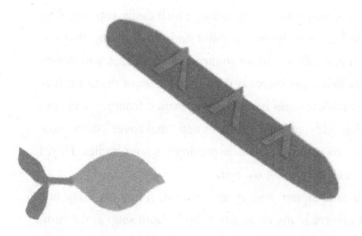

ORDINARY DAY

~ BREAKFAST ~

Glass of water

Grandma Louise's Oatmeal with Grated Apple

Slice of toasted whole wheat bread, buttered

Coffee or tea

~ LUNCH ~

Carrot and Orange Soup

Shrimp and Fennel Salad

½ cup yogurt and ½ grapefruit

Noncaloric beverage (or glass of white wine, but no wine at dinner)

~ DINNER ~

A few green olives (as an hors d'oeuvre and appetizer substitute)

Roasted Chicken with Endives

1 pear, 2 squares dark chocolate

*Wine (optional): a glass of white (perhaps a New World Chardonnay)
or light or medium red (perhaps a Côtes-du-Rhône)*

GRANDMA LOUISE'S OATMEAL WITH GRATED APPLE

My grandmother's oatmeal, which made its way into FWDGF, *is my idea of how to start the day with a yummy healthy breakfast, and it was heartily endorsed. I admit I've made the oatmeal for dinner now and then, particularly when I am alone and don't have much choice in the fridge.*

1 cup old-fashioned oatmeal

2⅓ cups water

Pinch of salt

1 medium apple, coarsely grated

½ teaspoon lemon juice

⅓ cup milk, whole or 2%

½ teaspoon butter

Brown sugar (or maple syrup) for serving

1. Combine the oatmeal, water, and salt. Bring to a boil.

2. Add the apple and lemon juice and cook for about 5 minutes, stirring occasionally.

3. Finish cooking by adding the milk and butter. Stir well. Serve immediately with a splash of brown sugar or a drizzle of maple syrup.

CARROT AND ORANGE SOUP

• SERVES 6 TO 8 •

· ·

4 tablespoons (½ stick)
  unsalted butter

½ large onion, peeled and
  chopped

1 pound carrots, peeled and
  chopped

Zest of 1 orange

1 medium potato, peeled
  and chopped

4 cups chicken broth or water

½ cup milk, whole or 2%

Salt and freshly ground
  pepper

1. Melt the butter in a large pot over medium-high heat. Add the onion and sauté until softened, 4 to 5 minutes.

2. Add the carrots, orange zest, potato, and chicken broth and bring to a boil. Cover, lower the heat, and simmer until the vegetables are tender, about 30 minutes.

3. Carefully transfer the mixture to a food mill or blender and purée until smooth. Add the milk and season to taste. This soup may be served hot or chilled.

SHRIMP AND FENNEL SALAD

• SERVES 4 •

· ·

1 shallot, minced

2 tablespoons lemon juice

1 teaspoon fennel seeds

1 tablespoon sherry vinegar

4 tablespoons olive oil

Salt and freshly ground
*   pepper*

2 fennel bulbs, trimmed,
*   cored, and thinly sliced*

8 ounces medium shrimp,
*   cooked and peeled*

1 apple, peeled, cored, and
*   diced*

1. In a small bowl, combine the shallot, lemon juice, fennel seeds, and sherry vinegar. Whisk in the olive oil and season to taste.

2. In a medium serving bowl, combine the fennel, shrimp, and apple. Add the dressing and gently toss. Serve at once.

ROASTED CHICKEN
WITH ENDIVES

• SERVES 4 •

1 (4-pound) free-range
chicken

2 lemons

1 tablespoon olive oil

Salt and freshly ground
pepper

1 large red onion, peeled
and thinly sliced

¼ cup peeled and coarsely
chopped shallots

1 cup white wine (or dry
vermouth)

2 tablespoons unsalted
butter

4 endives, washed, dried,
and quartered

1. Preheat the oven to 450 degrees.

2. Rinse the chicken and pat dry. Slice 1 lemon and place inside the cavity. Rub the outside of the chicken with olive oil and season all over (including the cavity). Place the chicken in a roasting pan, place the pan in the oven, and cook for 30 minutes.

3. Reduce the temperature to 350 degrees and continue cooking for 15 minutes. Add the onion and shallots to the roasting pan and continue cooking for another 15 minutes.

4. Add the white wine to the roasting pan, reduce the temperature to 300 degrees, and cook for an additional 30 minutes or until the juices run clear when the chicken is pierced with a fork. The total cooking time is about 1½ hours.

5. While the chicken roasts, melt 1 tablespoon butter in a skillet over medium-high heat and brown the endives on both sides, about 5 minutes.

continued on next page

Press the juice of 1 lemon and add to the endives. Season to taste, reduce the heat to medium-low, and continue cooking until the endives are tender, about 10 minutes.

6. Remove the chicken from the oven and reserve the juices from both the chicken and endives. Strain the combined juices into a small saucepan. Skim the fat and simmer over medium-high heat until slightly reduced, 3 to 5 minutes. Stir in the remaining tablespoon of butter and season to taste.

7. Carve the chicken into pieces and arrange on a serving platter surrounded by the endives. Serve family style accompanied by sauce.

LIGHT WORK DAY

BREAKFAST

Glass of water

Granola with ½ banana and 2% milk

Slivers of 1 or 2 cheeses (such as Gruyère or Cantal or Parmesan)

Coffee or tea

LUNCH

Velouté of Haricots Verts with Peppers and Ham

Bruschetta with Escarole

½ cup yogurt with berries

Noncaloric beverage

DINNER

Leeks and Onion Parmesan

Roasted Daurade (Sea Bream) with Vegetables

Tarte au Chocolat

Wine: a glass of Chardonnay or in warm weather a still rosé

VELOUTÉ OF HARICOTS VERTS WITH PEPPERS AND HAM

• SERVES 4 TO 6 •

1 tablespoon olive oil

2 medium shallots, peeled and chopped

2 garlic cloves, peeled and chopped

2 bell peppers (mix of red, orange, or yellow), seeded and chopped

2 medium potatoes, peeled and diced

1 pound haricots verts (fresh or frozen)

6 cups water

Salt and freshly ground pepper

2 tablespoons crème fraîche

3 ounces low-salt boiled ham, cut into small dice

2 tablespoons finely minced fresh parsley

1. Heat the olive oil in a large pot over medium heat. Add the shallots and garlic and sauté until fragrant and softened, about 2 minutes. Add the peppers and sauté another minute. Add the potatoes, haricots verts, and water and bring to a boil. Cover, reduce the heat, and simmer for 20 minutes or until the vegetables are tender.

2. Carefully transfer the cooked vegetables to a blender and add just enough of the cooking liquid to blend to the desired consistency. Season to taste.

3. This soup may be served warm or chilled. Before serving, add the crème fraîche and stir well. Garnish with the ham and parsley and serve.

BRUSCHETTA WITH ESCAROLE

• SERVES 4 •

1 head escarole

3 tablespoons olive oil plus additional for bread

2 tablespoons lemon juice

Salt and freshly ground pepper

3 teaspoons white wine vinegar

1 tablespoon golden raisins

4 slices country bread

1 garlic clove, peeled and halved

1 teaspoon finely minced fresh rosemary

1 tablespoon pine nuts, lightly toasted

1. Preheat the oven to 425 degrees.

2. Trim the outer leaves of the escarole and split into quarters. Rinse well and pat dry. Heat 1 tablespoon olive oil in a large skillet over medium-high heat and add the escarole. Cook, stirring, until it begins to wilt, about 5 minutes. Add the lemon juice and season to taste.

3. In a small bowl, combine the vinegar and raisins and set aside.

4. Lightly brush the bread with olive oil, rub with the cut side of the garlic, and lightly season with salt. Place directly on the oven rack and toast lightly, about 6 minutes.

5. Meanwhile, in a small bowl, whisk together the rosemary, vinegar and raisins, pine nuts, and the remaining 2 tablespoons olive oil. Season to taste.

6. To serve, place one quarter of the escarole on each toast and spoon the vinaigrette on top.

LEEKS AND ONION PARMESAN

• SERVES 4 •

6 leeks, white parts and 1 to
    2 inches of green, washed
2 tablespoons butter
2 tablespoons olive oil
Salt and freshly ground
    pepper
3 large red onions, peeled
    and thinly sliced
1 teaspoon lemon juice
¼ teaspoon fennel seeds
Pinch of freshly grated
    nutmeg
2 ounces Parmesan
2 tablespoons chopped fresh
    parsley

1. Cut each leek in half lengthwise and slice each half into thin strips. In a skillet, heat 1 tablespoon of butter and 1 tablespoon of olive oil over medium-low heat and sauté the leeks until soft, 12 to 15 minutes. Season to taste.

2. Meanwhile, in a separate skillet, heat the remaining tablespoon butter and olive oil and cook the onions until soft, about 10 minutes. Deglaze the pan with the lemon juice, stir in the fennel seeds and nutmeg, and season to taste.

3. To serve, place the warm leeks at the bottom of each plate. Cover with the sautéed onions and garnish with shavings of Parmesan (using a vegetable peeler) and chopped parsley.

ROASTED *DAURADE* (SEA BREAM) WITH VEGETABLES

• SERVES 4 •

3 onions, peeled and sliced

3 potatoes, peeled and sliced

2 yellow peppers, peeled and sliced

4 tomatoes, peeled and sliced

4 tablespoons olive oil

Salt and freshly ground pepper

4 (4- to 5-ounce) sea bream fillets

Juice of 1 lemon

½ cup chopped fresh cilantro

1 lemon, sliced

1. Preheat the oven to 400 degrees.

2. Place the onions, potatoes, yellow peppers, and tomatoes in a baking dish. Add 2 tablespoons olive oil, toss to combine, and season to taste. Cover the dish with foil, place in the oven, and bake until the vegetables are tender and a bit caramelized, about 30 minutes.

3. Uncover the baking dish, add the fillets, and pour the remaining 2 tablespoons olive oil and lemon juice over the fish and vegetables. Season to taste and continue cooking, uncovered, until the vegetables are tender, about 8 minutes.

4. Remove from the oven and serve immediately, garnished with cilantro and lemon slices.

TARTE AU CHOCOLAT

• MAKES ONE 9-INCH TART •

* *

1 recipe pâte brisée or pie dough (store-bought or homemade) for 9-inch pie

6 ounces dark chocolate (70 to 80% cacao preferred), chopped

⅓ cup 2% or whole milk

⅓ cup heavy cream

4 tablespoons sugar

4 egg yolks

1. Preheat the oven to 400 degrees.

2. Line a 9-inch tart pan with the pastry dough. Prick the bottom of the dough with a fork and cover the dough with foil, crimping the foil over the edges of the mold. Add dry beans or pellets and bake for 10 minutes. Remove the beans or pellets and foil and cook for another 5 minutes or until the tart shell is lightly golden. Remove from the oven and cool.

3. Lower the oven temperature to 275 degrees. Place the chocolate in a double boiler insert set above simmering water over medium heat and melt, stirring occasionally.

4. Meanwhile, place the milk, cream, and sugar in a small heavy saucepan and bring to a simmer over low heat, whisking to dissolve the sugar. Remove from the heat and add the milk-cream mixture to the melted chocolate, stirring until smooth. Set aside and allow to cool a bit before whisking in the egg yolks.

5. Pour the chocolate mixture into the tart shell and bake for 20 minutes or until the filling is just set. Remove from the oven and cool before unmolding and serving.

FISH DAY

BREAKFAST

Glass of water

Lemon Ricotta Pancakes

Coffee or tea

LUNCH

Avocado-Apple Salad with Gambas

Red snapper en Papillote

Yogurt with Crème Chocolat

DINNER

Scallop "Ceviche" with Mango and Parmesan

Skate à la Grenobloise

Cheese platter

Apricot Tart

Wine: a glass of Sancerre or other fruity but dry white

LEMON RICOTTA PANCAKES

• SERVES 4 TO 6 •

4 tablespoons unsalted
butter, melted

6 eggs, separated

1½ cups fresh ricotta

¼ cup white flour

¼ cup whole wheat flour

⅓ cup sugar

Zest of 2 lemons (Meyer
preferred)

1 tablespoon poppy seeds
(optional)

Maple syrup (or honey) for
serving

1. Mix all the ingredients except the egg whites until just combined.

2. Beat the egg whites to soft peaks and gently fold into the mixture.

3. Heat a large nonstick skillet over medium heat. Spoon the batter by tablespoonfuls (I prefer mini sizes—it feels like more when it is actually less) into the hot skillet, and when holes appear in the pancakes, flip them and cook for another minute or two, until golden. Repeat until all the batter is used. Serve immediately with a drizzle of maple syrup or honey.

AVOCADO-APPLE SALAD
WITH GAMBAS

8 large shrimp in the shell

Salt and freshly ground
  pepper

3 tablespoons olive oil

Juice of 2 limes

2 ripe avocados, peeled and
  sliced

2 Granny Smith apples,
  rinsed and cut into
  matchsticks

¼ cup fresh cilantro,
  roughly chopped

1. Season the shrimp to taste. Heat 1 tablespoon olive oil in a large skillet over medium heat, add the shrimp, reduce the heat, and cook over medium-low heat for 10 minutes. Remove from the heat and reserve.

2. In a large bowl, whisk together the lime juice with the remaining 2 tablespoons olive oil. Add the sliced avocados and apples, season to taste, and gently toss.

3. Peel the shrimp, keeping the tails on. Add the shrimp to the salad and garnish with the cilantro. Serve immediately.

RED SNAPPER *EN PAPILLOTE*

1 teaspoon olive oil plus
   additional for parchment
   paper
2 medium tomatoes, rinsed
   and thinly sliced
1 lemon, rinsed and thinly
   sliced
1 zucchini, rinsed and cut
   into matchsticks
Salt and freshly ground
   pepper
4 (4- to 5-ounce) red
   snapper fillets
1 cup fresh lemon verbena
   leaves
Fleur de sel

1. Preheat the oven to 375 degrees.

2. Cut four pieces of parchment paper into 12- x 16-inch rectangles and brush the centers with olive oil. Place one quarter of the tomato and lemon slices and zucchini matchsticks in the center of the first piece of parchment paper and season to taste. Top with 1 red snapper fillet, ¼ cup verbena leaves, and a drizzle of olive oil, and season to taste. Seal the packet by bringing up the sides to the center and folding down tightly. Seal the ends by folding each in tightly. Repeat with the remaining ingredients, creating four packets.

3. Place the packets on a baking sheet and bake for 12 to 15 minutes. Open, sprinkle with fleur de sel, and serve immediately.

YOGURT WITH *CRÈME CHOCOLAT*

••

¼ cup heavy cream

4 ounces dark chocolate (70% to 80% cacao preferred), finely chopped

2 cups plain Greek-style yogurt

1. Heat the cream in a small saucepan over low heat until it reaches a simmer. Place the chocolate in a medium bowl and pour the hot cream over the chocolate. Let stand for 2 minutes, then stir until smooth.

2. Divide the yogurt evenly among four small bowls and top with the chocolate cream. Serve immediately.

SCALLOP "CEVICHE" WITH MANGO AND PARMESAN

• SERVES 4 •

- -

8 medium sea scallops, tough muscles removed and each cut horizontally into 4 slices

1 tablespoon lemon juice

Salt and freshly ground pepper

½ ripe mango, peeled and cut into matchsticks

1 ounce Parmesan, shaved using a vegetable peeler

1 teaspoon extra virgin olive oil

1. In a medium bowl, gently toss the sliced scallops with lemon juice and season to taste.

2. Slightly overlap 8 slices of scallops in a circle on each plate. Place a small amount of mango in the center of the circle and top with a few shavings of Parmesan. Drizzle with olive oil and season to taste. Serve immediately.

SKATE *À LA GRENOBLOISE*

• SERVES 4 •

1½ pounds potatoes, peeled and cut into ½-inch dice

Salt and freshly ground pepper

4 (7-ounce) boned skate wings

¼ cup unbleached all-purpose flour

6 tablespoons unsalted butter

⅓ cup capers, drained

4 slices baguette or country bread, cut into ¼-inch dice and sautéed in butter until golden

½ cup finely chopped fresh parsley

1 lemon, sliced

1. Place the diced potatoes in a steamer insert set over a pot of boiling water and cook for 12 minutes or until soft. Season to taste and keep warm.

2. Season the skate wings with salt and pepper and dredge in the flour, shaking off any excess. Melt 2 tablespoons butter in a large nonstick skillet over medium-high heat and cook the skate until golden brown and just cooked through, about 3 minutes per side.

3. Remove the skate from the pan and melt the remaining 4 tablespoons butter, swirling the pan, until the butter begins to brown and smell slightly nutty. Quickly remove the skillet from the heat and add the capers (be careful; the butter may splatter).

4. Place one piece of skate and some steamed potatoes on each plate. Spoon the butter-caper sauce over the skate and sprinkle with the croûtons and chopped parsley. Garnish with lemon slices and serve immediately.

APRICOT TART

. . . .

Marsha, an American friend who lives in our village in Provence, was proud to announce that she had learned a new word, chapelure, *from her French friends who love to bake. She was making lots of fruit tarts from the abundance of local fruits at our village market, but she felt her open-top pies were too juicy and messy. So her neighbors suggested she make a* chapelure, *which refers mostly to a coating for savory dishes to prevent them from "falling apart," but anyone local knew what it meant with regard to making a tart. The trick with a fruit tart is to add a mix of ground almonds with a bit of sugar and spread it on the dough, thus providing a binding and structure for fruit that is then added on top. After baking the dough and apricots, just sprinkle a bit of sugar on top of the tart when it comes out of the oven. As the apricot season is one of the shortest of the fruit seasons, I always look forward to it and my annual apricot "cure" (a fruit-only diet orgy), which includes an apricot tart, to which I add some slivers of almond on top.*

1 recipe pâte brisée (store-bought or homemade) for a 9-inch tart

½ cup blanched almonds, finely ground

¼ cup plus 2 teaspoons sugar

1½ to 2 pounds fresh apricots, rinsed, cut in halves, and pitted

2 teaspoons honey

3 tablespoons slivered almonds, lightly toasted

Crème fraîche (optional)

1. Preheat the oven to 400 degrees. On a lightly floured surface roll the dough to an 11-inch round. Transfer to an 9-inch fluted tart pan with a removable bottom. Prick the dough lining the bottom of the pan with a fork. Cover and chill for 10 minutes. Place the tart in the oven and par-bake for 10 minutes. Remove from the oven and reduce the temperature to 375 degrees.

2. In a food processor, combine the blanched almonds and ¼ cup sugar and pulse just until the almonds are finely ground. Spread the mixture evenly over the bottom of the tart. Place the apricot

halves, cut side down, on top, slightly overlapping. Drizzle with honey, place in the oven, and bake for 40 minutes or until the crust is lightly browned.

3. Remove from the oven and sprinkle with the slivered almonds and 2 teaspoons sugar. Serve warm or at room temperature with slightly sweetened crème fraîche, if desired.

VARIATION: *Other wonderful fruit tart options include peaches (or a mix of peaches and nectarines) with pistachio nuts instead of almonds, plums with lemon zest and cherries, or Italian plums with a dash of cinnamon.*

VALENTINE'S DAY DINNER

I always assumed that Valentine's Day was the biggest restaurant night for most couples. Sort of easy and still a rewarding way to celebrate—like guys buying girls flowers. It turns out Mother's Day is the big restaurant day, which makes sense—take Mom out of the kitchen for a day, no prepping, cooking, or cleaning for her at home (and easy on the kids and husband, plenty of food choices, and signing a credit card is the only hand labor involved). Valentine's Day is still a strong restaurant occasion, but as someone who ate in restaurants three hundred times a year during my Champagne career, dining home was special, dining out was not (often it was plain work). And since for me cooking is an act of love, I like to stay home and celebrate Valentine's Day with a tête-à-tête dinner. I would cook up some of our special and not-everyday favorites and Edward would pick out a special bottle of wine. I appreciate that for some people, an assortment of children can get in the way sometimes, but surely there are occasional workarounds when, eventually or initially, there are no children around and Valentine's Day evening can be that very special romantic meal—corny to some but it remains a tradition, ritual, and renewal that is pleasurable, symbolic, and healthy. I recommend it. You might even consider the planning, preparation, and sharing that goes into making the meal a success a kind of gustatory foreplay.

HORS D'OEUVRE: *Domestic caviar on toasts*

MAIN COURSE: *Duck Breasts* à la Gasconne *with Wild Rice*

SALAD COURSE À LA FRANÇAISE: *Salad of greens with lemon and olive oil dressing (avoid vinegar when serving a good wine)*

CHEESE COURSE: *Slivers of three goat cheeses*

DESSERT: *Classic Chocolate Mousse*

WINE: *Champagne (or sparkling wine) to start, then a Pinot Noir or a rosé Champagne throughout the meal*

DUCK BREASTS *À LA GASCONNE* WITH WILD RICE

• SERVES 2 •

Pinch of coarse salt

Pinch of crumbled bay leaves

Pinch of crumbled dried thyme leaves

½ teaspoon chopped fresh parsley

1 garlic clove, peeled and sliced

¼ teaspoon finely minced shallots

4 peppercorns, coarsely crushed

2 (4- to 6-ounce) duck magrets (breasts)

1 cup wild rice

1. In a large baking pan, mix the salt, bay leaves, thyme, parsley, garlic, shallots, and peppercorns. Roll the magrets in the mixture and spread them out, skin side up.

2. Cover with plastic and refrigerate the duck breasts for 24 hours, turning once.

3. Cook the wild rice according to the package directions. Drain and keep warm.

4. Remove the duck breasts from the marinade. Wipe or rinse to remove any excess seasoning; pat dry. Score the skin (so fat can render during cooking) diagonally at 1-inch intervals with a sharp knife to create a diamond pattern. (Discard the marinade.) Arrange the duck breasts, skin side down, on the broiler rack (4 inches away from the heat). Broil for 1 to 2 minutes; turn over and broil for 3 to 4 minutes. The magrets should be medium-rare.

5. Place on a carving board and let rest for 2 to 3 minutes. Thinly slice the duck breast meat crosswise on the bias and serve on top of the wild rice.

CLASSIC CHOCOLATE MOUSSE

• SERVES 4 •

6 ounces dark chocolate
  (70% to 80% cacao
  preferred), chopped
2 tablespoons unsalted
  butter, cut into small
  pieces
4 medium egg whites
Pinch of salt
2 tablespoons sugar
½ cup heavy cream, chilled
1 teaspoon pure vanilla
  extract
Whipped cream and shaved
  chocolate (optional)

1. In a double boiler set over barely simmering water, melt the chocolate, stirring until smooth. Remove from the heat, stir in the butter, and let the chocolate cool until it's slightly warm but not hot to the touch.

2. In a mixing bowl, combine the egg whites and salt and beat until soft peaks form. Add the sugar and continue whisking until the egg whites form stiff, glossy peaks. Place the whipped egg whites in a large bowl and gently fold in a small amount of warm chocolate. Once incorporated, add the remaining chocolate, being careful not to over-mix.

3. Place the chilled cream and vanilla in a clean mixing bowl and whip the cream until soft peaks form. Gently fold the whipped cream into the chocolate mixture in two batches. Divide the chocolate mousse among four dessert bowls and chill for 2 hours and up to 1 day. Remove from the refrigerator and let stand at room temperature for 20 minutes before serving. Chocolate mousse may be garnished with additional whipped cream and shaved chocolate, if desired.

NOTE: *Chocolate mousse for four on Valentine's Day? What kind of romance is that? The proper recipe calls for preparation of a portion larger than for two. So, compliments of the chef, eat the second portion the next day or two. Enjoy.*

BRUNCH FOR 4 OR 8

(DOUBLE INGREDIENTS FOR 8)

Selection of cereal and fruit

Selection of breads and mini viennoiseries
(croissants, brioche, and pains au chocolat*)*

Scrambled Eggs with Herbs and Smoked Salmon—Bacon Toast

Crab Tartines *Avocado*

Coffee and tea

Sparkling wine or Champagne (optional)

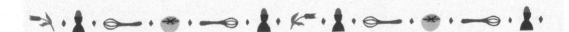

SCRAMBLED EGGS WITH HERBS AND SMOKED SALMON–BACON TOAST

• SERVES 4 •

8 eggs

Salt and freshly ground
pepper

1 tablespoon butter

1 teaspoon water

1 tablespoon crème fraîche

2 tablespoons minced fresh
parsley

2 tablespoons minced fresh
chives

1 teaspoon minced fresh dill

3 slices bacon

4 slices country whole wheat
bread, toasted and
buttered

4 slices smoked salmon

1. In a medium bowl, whisk the eggs together and season to taste. Melt the butter with 1 teaspoon water in a double boiler insert set over barely simmering water. Add the eggs and cook, stirring until thickened and just cooked through, about 6 minutes. Do not overcook, as you want the eggs to remain soft and creamy. Remove from the heat and stir in the crème fraîche and herbs. Keep warm.

2. In a sauté pan over medium-high heat, cook the bacon until crisp. Remove the bacon from the pan and drain on paper towels.

3. Place the buttered toasts horizontally on a cutting board and remove the crusts. Cover the top of each toast with 1 slice of salmon and cut each vertically into 3 *mouillettes* ("fingers"). Place 3 *mouillettes* on each plate and top with pieces of bacon, breaking the bacon to fit each *mouillette* as necessary. Spoon the eggs onto the plates and serve immediately.

CRAB *TARTINES* AVOCADO

• SERVES 4 •

1 ripe avocado, pitted and
   peeled

2 tablespoons lemon juice

½ teaspoon ground cumin

⅛ teaspoon hot sauce

1 garlic clove, peeled and
   chopped

1 small onion, peeled and
   chopped

½ medium tomato, diced

1 teaspoon minced fresh
   cilantro

Salt and freshly ground
   pepper

1 pink grapefruit

4 slices country bread,
   lightly toasted

8 ounces crabmeat, picked
   over for shells and
   cartilage, shredded

1. Place the avocado, lemon juice, cumin, hot sauce, garlic, and onion in a food processor and blend until smooth. Fold in the tomato and cilantro, season to taste, and reserve in the refrigerator, covered, if not using immediately.

2. To prepare the grapefruit segments, cut slices off the top and bottom of the grapefruit and then slice away the peel and pith, top to bottom, following the curve of the fruit. Working over a bowl and using a small, sharp knife, cut between the membranes to release the segments.

3. To serve, spread toasted bread slices with the avocado mixture. Top with the shredded crabmeat, garnish with the grapefruit slices, and cut each *tartine* diagonally.

Chapter Seven

ONCE IN A WHILE A LITTLE CHAMPAGNE

I recently had a couple from Brazil for lunch in Provence. After five years of living in Paris, they were getting ready to head back to São Paulo. While they had been to Provence before, they had not been to our corner of paradise, and I took them to the traditional Friday morning outdoor market (as in a centuries-old traditional village market) to shop for lunch. I was not surprised in the least when they chose a rotisserie chicken for their main dish. My guests often do, and so do I. There's a guy there (*c'est un phénomène,* as the French expression for a character goes) who roasts certified organic chickens in a specially built truck and rotisserie oven. Delicious. Typically French, he won't share the ingredients for the sauce, which definitely has olive oil, salt, herbes de Provence, and green olives. The secret ingredient is an enigma. We try to find out but to no avail.

At home, I quickly made some ratatouille from the market vegetables to go with the chicken, offered some local olives and thin slices of *saucisson* as a nibble in the kitchen as I prepared things, and set the outdoor table. "What would you like to drink?" I asked. With this you can have a white, rosé, or red wine, or, of course, Champagne. The woman did not hesitate: Champagne.

Often in the spring in New York City, we throw a big cocktail party at our home and it goes on for hours inside the apartment and especially out on the terrace, with people coming and going. It is our chance to say hello to a lot of friends before people's summer plans take control of their lives, and for us that means less time in Manhattan to connect with friends. Each time we host the party, Edward insists we have bottles of a red wine on hand—usually a light Burgundy—along with sparkling and still waters and plenty of Champagne. Each year, no one drinks the red wine, but there are plenty of empty bottles of Champagne after the party. In my experience, it is indeed the rare person who shuns a glass of the foaming grape from Eastern France (Tennyson's term, not mine).

Champagne really is magic in a bottle. It is a great wine, tasty, refreshing, complex, but more than that: Champagne is a state of mind. It connotes at once carefree, celebratory, festive, and, yes, bubbly overtones. It is a great mood enhancer. To my ears, the pop of a Champagne (or sparkling wine) cork launches a festive mood of pleasure and celebration. No occasion is too small. And it is also a great and versatile food wine. In my profession, I was never shy about offering Champagne before, during, and after a meal. *Bien sûr,* I often offered a dinner *tout au Champagne,* only with the wines of Champagne served with each course. It is a recipe for success. So, I offer now two menus that marry well with Champagne and some additional tried and tested food ideas. And why in a book with not getting fat in its title? Champagne is a food that is both comparatively healthy and nonfattening, and that will become clearer. Also as Madame de Pompadour remarked, "Champagne is the only wine which leaves a woman beautiful after drinking it."

I've found two reasons why people are sometimes reluctant to offer Champagne or sparkling wine. They are uncomfortable or afraid to open a bottle, and they think Champagne gives you a headache (wrong, unless perhaps you over-indulge, but that's true of any alcoholic beverage). Before I address and hopefully dismiss both those reservations, let's get on the same page with some Champagne basics.

Types and Styles

Here's a little primer to help you select and serve Champagne from France, which is a blended wine made of grapes from vineyards spread across a highly restricted and regulated region and only from Pinot Noir, Pinot Meunier, and Chardonnay grapes—mostly in combination but sometimes singly. There is *vintage* and *non-vintage* Champagne. When there is an exceptional harvest—perhaps three or four times in a decade—all wines used in the blend come from that harvest and its year appears on the bottle's label. The style and character of each vintage Champagne varies from vintage to vintage and from house to house (which, of course, source grapes from different vineyards and have different percentages of grape types in their blends). Most Champagne, however, is the less expensive non-vintage, which is made from a blend of wines from a given year plus reserve wines of various ages.

The blending maintains a consistently distinctive house "taste" from year to year, so that the style and character of a non-vintage Champagne does not vary from year to year, only from house to house. House styles vary from light to medium to full bodied, depending, among other things, upon the percentage of Chardonnay grape in the house blend. Generally, the more Chardonnay, the lighter the style wine. The House of Veuve Clicquot, for example, uses Chardonnay for only about a third of its blend, and thus the house style is full-bodied.

Most Champagnes are dry, indeed bone dry, and labeled *brut,* but to others more sugar is added and the resultant sweeter Champagne is, ironically, called extra dry. Even sweeter, it is called demi-sec (half dry). These sweeter styles of Champagne go well with some foods, but are generally reserved for desserts. Four other types and styles require a bit of quaffing to develop personal preferences and can be found in non-vintage and vintage versions but not from every house. A favorite "food wine" of mine is rosé Champagne, usually made by the addition of some still red wine during the blending process. Another type is *blanc de blancs* Champagne, a blend of only Chardonnay grapes, and the lightest of Champagnes. A *crémant* is a Champagne with slightly less effervescence, and not commonly produced; however, the word *crémant* is widely used to identify a great many sparkling wines from outside the Champagne region. Confused? Most Champagne houses also produce a "best we can make" Champagne, which they put in fancy bottles and charge more for than their other types and styles: They are the so-called prestige *cuvées* or *têtes de cuvée.* Again, these are a matter of personal preference (including price), and you sometimes have to bring a lot to the tasting experience to fully appreciate the taste nuances, subtleties, and rarities that help justify the prices, but they are certainly painstakingly made over many years before being released. Most, including Dom Pérignon, Cristal, and La Grande Dame, are only made in vintage years, but perhaps the most esteemed of all, Krug, is produced each year and is identified as MV for multi-vintage.

Opening the Bottle (or Two)

Opening a bottle is *très facile.* I learned to do it, and countless number of times I demonstrated to women and men in all sorts of settings—from restaurant staff sessions to cooking schools to live TV shows—the proper and safe way to open a bottle. Growing up with a mother whose favorite beverage was Champagne, I saw lots and lots of cork popping in our home. My mother was a champion at opening bottles and toasting, so more often than not she was the one who did it all and then passed on the bottle to my father, who would do the pouring.

Chill the bottle properly before serving; the ideal temperature is 46 to 48 degrees. Twenty minutes in a bucket filled with ice and water or several hours in a refrigerator should cool the wine sufficiently.

If the bottle is wet, dry it off. To open, remove the cap foil and untwist the wire muzzle. You can completely remove the wire muzzle then or leave it draped over the cork. If you do take it off, beware—the cork can on occasion shoot out from the pressure in the bottle alone. Holding the cork (with loosened wire muzzle) firmly with one hand and generally with your thumb on top of the cork, point the bottle on a slight angle away from you or anyone else. Then with your other hand around the bottle's base or waist, slowly turn the bottle in one direction. The operative phase is "turn the bottle, not the cork." The cork will come out easily with a soft "pop" (or sigh) and without loss of froth, sparkle, or wine. Tulip or flute glasses should be filled about two thirds.

Once the cork is popped, it is hard to resist sharing the entire contents of the bottle, but if there's Champagne left, it can be maintained in the refrigerator for a day or two, depending on how much air versus wine is in the bottle *if* you recork the bottle in some fashion to keep the bubbles (CO_2) in and extra air (oxygen) out. Like most wines, exposure to oxygen causes oxidation in Champagne and the wine's flavors and complexity fade into oblivion, not instantly but gradually. So, the more air versus wine in a bottle, the less time it will survive at its peak flavor. Champagne, if kept under pressure, stays pretty well. And an inexpensive "Champagne recorker" (a plug with clasps to grab the neck of the bottle) is widely available and a good investment, though other stoppers work fine, even plastic wrap. I have a host of recorkers, mostly unused.

As for headaches, quality Champagne and sparkling wines are low in histamines and unless you have a special condition where alcoholic beverages of any kind trigger headaches including migraines, you should be fine. The same claim cannot be made for cheap sparklers made from different grapes and with different methods and having higher amounts of sugar. Champagne is a very dry (meaning not sweet) wine. Of course, it is bubbly, and that sometimes means it goes to your head a little quicker than a still wine, especially on an empty stomach, but lots of people enjoy the charms it brings to their head. It is, by the way, comparatively low in calories. A 4- or 5-ounce serving is less than 90 calories, and usually a pour of Champagne is about 3 ounces, perhaps 4. It is bubbly, and some people do not like the aggressiveness of carbonated beverages. Champagne is not in the same class; it does not have big bubbles pumped into it as do sodas and some sparkling waters. Its bubbles are tiny and smooth and the result of a natural double fermentation process. And others claim they don't like the acidity of Champagne. It is acidic, but not more than most dry wines.

Once the bottle is open, it's meant to be drunk, and that means some food is de rigueur. If nothing else is available, bread is a wonderful accompaniment to Champagne. You probably know the French saying, *vivre d'amour, de pain et d'eau fraîche*, to live with love, bread, and water . . . well, I learned to replace the water with the bubbly. Not a bad combination, don't you think?

CHICKEN *TOUT AU CHAMPAGNE* MENU

I was amused though not surprised when one of the recipes from French Women Don't Get Fat *that received the most feedback and favorable attention from readers all over the world was and is the chicken au Champagne. So, I'm including it in this first menu sample because it is easy, foolproof, and most of all delicious. It is one of my safe bets that I have placed time and time again. You can try the same dish with white wine or dry vermouth and the chicken will have a different taste. Whenever possible I stick to the bubbly as the magic ingredient and with bottle open, I have no-excuse number 23,438,408 for a meal* tout au Champagne.

APPETIZER
Poêlée *of Mushrooms*

MAIN COURSE
Chicken au Champagne

SIDE DISH
Stuffed Zucchini

DESSERT
Baked Apples with Lemon Cream

CHAMPAGNE
non-vintage brut or a non-vintage or vintage rosé throughout

POÊLÉE OF MUSHROOMS

· SERVES 4 ·

· ·

1 tablespoon olive oil

1 tablespoon unsalted butter

1 shallot, peeled and minced

1 pound assorted mushrooms (use 3 varieties such as morels, crimini, shiitake, oyster, or portobello), cleaned and sliced

1 teaspoon lemon juice

Salt and freshly ground pepper

2 tablespoons chopped fresh parsley

1. In a large skillet, heat the olive oil and butter over medium heat. Add the shallot and sauté until fragrant, about 1 minute.

2. Add the mushrooms and lemon juice, season to taste, and sauté for 8 to 10 minutes until cooked. Remove from the heat, sprinkle with fresh parsley, and serve.

CHICKEN *AU CHAMPAGNE*

4 chicken breasts (with skin and bone)

Salt and freshly ground pepper

Chervil, tarragon, or thyme (optional)

1 cup Champagne (Veuve Clicquot Yellow Label Brut recommended)

1 shallot, quartered

Cooked brown rice for serving

1. Place the chicken breasts in a roasting pan and season them. Pour ½ cup of the Champagne over the breasts. Make a slit in each breast and insert a piece of shallot.

2. Place the pan under the broiler, skin side down, for 3 minutes, until the skin is nicely browned. Turn and broil the other side for 5 minutes.

3. Remove the chicken from the broiler, baste with the pan juices, and add the remaining ½ cup Champagne. Add additional herb, if using. Adjust the oven temperature to 475 degrees and bake the chicken for 30 minutes, basting once or twice.

4. Serve over brown rice. Pour the cooking juices from the chicken over the meat and rice. Serve the remainder of the bottle of Champagne (about 6 glasses) with the meal.

STUFFED ZUCCHINI

• SERVES 4 •

4 small round zucchini (if you can't find round, it's okay to use 4 small standard zucchini)

Salt and freshly ground pepper

1 tablespoon olive oil

2 garlic cloves, peeled and minced

1 large onion, peeled and finely chopped

¾ pound ground beef

¾ cup cooked rice

½ cup grated Parmesan

1 egg, beaten

1 (14.5-ounce) can diced tomatoes

2 tablespoons minced fresh parsley

1 cup tomato sauce

1. Preheat the oven to 375 degrees. Cut the stem and flower ends off the zucchini and cut each in half lengthwise. Using a grapefruit spoon or melon baller, scoop out and discard most of the zucchini flesh and seeds, leaving an even ½ inch of flesh attached to the skin. Season inside with salt and pepper and set aside.

2. Heat the olive oil in a medium nonstick sauté pan over medium-high heat and sauté the garlic and onion until softened, about 4 minutes. Add the ground beef and cook until the meat is no longer pink and starts to brown. Remove from the heat, carefully drain, and place in a mixing bowl.

3. When the onion-beef mixture is cool, add the rice, ¼ cup Parmesan, the egg, tomatoes, and parsley and mix to combine. Season to taste and fill the zucchini halves with stuffing.

4. Pour the tomato sauce into a baking dish just large enough to hold the zucchini and place the stuffed zucchini on top. Sprinkle the zucchini with the remaining Parmesan and bake for 40 minutes. Serve warm.

BAKED APPLES
WITH LEMON CREAM

• SERVES 4 •

2 firm baking apples, such as Cortland or Golden Delicious

2 lemons (preferably organic or Meyer)

1½ tablespoons unsalted butter plus additional for baking dish

4 tablespoons sugar

⅓ cup crème fraîche

1. Preheat the oven to 375 degrees. Rinse the apples and cut in half horizontally. Using a grapefruit spoon or melon baller, remove the core and seeds and sprinkle the cut sides with the juice of 1 lemon.

2. Lightly butter a baking dish and place the apple halves in it, cut side up. Sprinkle the apples with 1 tablespoon sugar, dot with butter, and bake for 20 to 25 minutes.

3. Wash the remaining lemon; grate the zest and press 3 tablespoons of juice. In a bowl, whip the crème fraîche with the remaining 3 tablespoons sugar, the lemon zest, and 3 tablespoons lemon juice. Cover and refrigerate until ready to serve.

4. Baked apples may be served warm or at room temperature. Garnish with a dollop of lemon cream.

A CHAMPAGNE
MEDLEY DINNER

⁓ HORS D'OEUVRE ⁓

Prosciutto Wrapped Around Grissini

CHAMPAGNE: *A non-vintage brut, my first thought, but perhaps a crémant or a blanc de blancs if you want to start off with a lighter, softer, and more uncommon touch*

⁓ APPETIZER ⁓

Scallops Maison Blanche

CHAMPAGNE: *Vintage*

⁓ MAIN COURSE ⁓

Duck Breasts with Pears

CHAMPAGNE: *Vintage rosé, preferably a full-bodied style and preferably 5 to 10 years old*

⁓ DESSERT ⁓

Strawberry Parfait

CHAMPAGNE: *Demi-sec*

⁓ NOTE ⁓

If you really want to splurge you can start with a prestige cuvée *Champagne, the top of the line, and progress from a younger vintage to an older one.*

PROSCIUTTO WRAPPED
AROUND GRISSINI

This doesn't require a recipe, of course, just a little serving tip. While you can perhaps make your own grissini—those addictive thin breadsticks—most people and restaurants I know buy them. And unless you own a farm with pigs, I don't recommend you make your own prosciutto (not that I imagine you ever thought of doing so), just buy some paper-thin slices. A quarter or half pound goes a very long way. Wrap a slice around one end of a breadstick so that a quarter to a half of the breadstick is covered and you have a great finger-food hors d'oeuvre, a bit like a lollipop or ice cream cone. I put the prosciutto end up, fanned out in a glass, and instead of finger food on a tray, I have a container in my hand to offer to guests. And sometimes, I simply strategically place a few of these around during aperitif time.

SCALLOPS *MAISON BLANCHE*

• SERVES 4 •

When the Obamas moved into the White House, like presidents and first ladies before them, their food and dining preferences got a good deal of attention, especially after Michelle Obama became a spokesperson for healthy eating and started a garden. The French ate this up and gave it a lot of media play. I also was in France during one of the Obamas' visit in the spring of 2009 and learned that the first lady loves spinach and the president loves scallops. I couldn't resist sharing one of my favorite marriages. So, voilà scallops (on a bed of greens) Maison Blanche. Perhaps someday they may be served in the White House . . . you never know.

2 teaspoons olive oil

2 pounds fresh spinach, washed and drained

Sea salt

12 medium sea scallops (about ¾ pound)

2 tablespoons lemon juice

1 tablespoon walnut oil

Fleur de sel

2 tablespoons chopped walnuts (optional)

1. Heat 1 teaspoon olive oil in a large, nonstick skillet over medium heat. Add the spinach, a pinch of sea salt, and cover and cook over medium-low heat for 5 minutes or until the spinach is slightly wilted and just cooked. Transfer to a plate and keep warm.

2. Pat the scallops dry. Heat the remaining teaspoon olive oil in the same skillet over medium-high heat and add the scallops. Add the lemon juice and sear 2 to 3 minutes on each side.

3. To serve, place one quarter of the spinach on each plate and top with three scallops. Drizzle with walnut oil and season with fleur de sel. Garnish with chopped walnuts, if using, and serve immediately.

DUCK BREASTS WITH PEARS

• SERVES 4 •

4 (6- to 7-ounce) duck
magrets (breasts)

Salt and freshly ground
pepper

2 ripe Comice pears, rinsed,
dried, cored, and cut
lengthwise into ¼-inch
slices

½ teaspoon Sichuan pepper

¼ cup balsamic vinegar

1. Pat the duck breasts dry and score the skin diagonally at 1-inch intervals with a sharp knife to create a diamond pattern (be careful not to cut into the meat); season both sides with salt and pepper.

2. Heat a large sauté pan over medium-high heat and add the duck breasts, skin side down. Cook for 8 minutes, allowing the fat to render and the skin to become crisp. Turn over, and cook for an additional 4 to 5 minutes for medium rare. Remove from the pan, cover, and rest for 10 minutes.

3. Pour off all but 2 tablespoons of duck fat and add the pear slices. Season with the Sichuan pepper and cook over medium-high heat until golden brown and crisp-tender, about 1½ minutes per side. Remove the pears from the pan and keep warm.

4. Deglaze the pan with balsamic vinegar and reduce until syrupy, about 45 seconds. Slice each duck breast crosswise into ½-inch-thick slices and fan on a plate. Drizzle with balsamic vinegar, garnish with pear slices, season to taste, and serve immediately.

NOTE: *Sichuan pepper may be difficult to find in the States, so a good substitution for this recipe is ½ teaspoon freshly ground pepper combined with a small pinch of crushed anise seed.*

STRAWBERRY PARFAIT

• SERVES 1 •

. . . .

½ cup fresh strawberries,
  rinsed, hulled, and sliced

½ teaspoon lemon juice

½ cup plain yogurt

Freshly ground pepper

1. In a small bowl, toss the strawberries with the lemon juice.

2. Using a parfait dish or other small glass dish, alternate layers of yogurt and strawberries, grinding a bit of fresh pepper on top of each layer of strawberries. Serve immediately.

More Food for Thought and Champagne

Bread and Champagne are for me a marriage made in Heaven, especially when the bread is a tad warm. Another similarly ambrosial combination is anything doughy, such as brioche, *gougères*, or puff pastry, served with Champagne, not indulgences you want to abuse but as a few bites as an aperitif, which should convince you Mae West was right when she said, "too much of a good thing . . . is wonderful." Alas, it is necessary portion control that proves that rule.

To me, however, seafood and fish are what I love best with my glass of bubbly. Oysters top my list, but really anything on the seafood platter from urchins to crabs to clams to scallops to mussels works for me. If going luxurious, without question lobster, that's a real treat, and I learned while living in New England that there is nothing better than just steaming the lobster, then serving it with some melted butter and a glass of bubbly. My American father of the day, a great seafood and bubbly lover, taught me that one. (I had never had fresh lobster before landing in New England and could have eaten it a few times a week.) And these days it's the special occasion treat I get going to the Union Square market in Manhattan and getting live lobster (females are best) trapped off Long Island.

Fish preparations, as long as they are not heavy on cream, are wonderful with Champagne and here my preferences are snapper, bass, *rouget* (red mullet), cod, skate, halibut, and turbot (the last only rarely ordered in restaurants), as well as local fish such as the river ones in Champagne called *sandre* (bream).

White meats are a great match with Champagne, whether the meat is chicken, Cornish hen, turkey, or veal. Cornish hen stuffed with brown rice, nuts, and golden raisins served with Champagne is one of Edward's favorite dishes.

As for veggies, mushrooms are the ideal marriage. When in France in the fall mushroom season, I love to sauté a few types of mushrooms with maybe an egg or omelet on the side, a slice of good sourdough bread, and a glass of bubbly. That's a perfect meal for me. In the spring, my all-time favorite fresh morels (but alas very expensive these days) would be my top choice. Cooked with a tiny bit of oil and butter, some shallots, and at the end a dash of cream and some fresh parsley very finely minced is a dish I would probably order on a desert island or as one of the last meals of my life.

For asparagus, artichokes, salads, and most cheeses, especially the pungent ones, skip Champagne, since its complex, elegant flavors will be overpowered. Stick to fresh goat cheese or light but not too creamy cheese types; my favorite Champagne and cheese pairing is with Parmesan (the fat and oiliness that makes it a good marriage). Slivers of Parmesan make for a simple hors d'oeuvre served with Champagne.

For red meat, I enjoy a rosé Champagne combo with duck and even lamb. Either is always a conversation piece, as not many people think of Champagne with red meat. A full-bodied rosé Champagne is Pinot Noir, after all.

To go a step further, steak and pizza also marry well with the bubbly. The fat/oil works well with the acidity in the bubbly. So often while on the lecture tour, people would come to me after the Q & A to admit their favorite combo was pizza and bubbly or steak and bubbly (lucky them), but they were embarrassed to ask the question in public because they thought it was a poor combo. To this, I'd say nonsense. (I now bring up and ask the question myself.) I'd also add, there is no stupid question and personal preferences generally win in the end. Anyway, pizza and bubbly and steak and bubbly are two of my favorite combinations. I was privileged to have to drink Champagne with so many foods (and not to have to pay for the Champagne myself) to discover these special tastes—and a few more.

Popular perception to the contrary, Champagne is not the most dessert-friendly wine. What wines are? Mostly sweet wines, and a demi-sec Champagne works, but as with most sweet wines the sweetness alongside sweetness does not contrast or flatter either. (They are often better just by themselves.) And the dryness and comparatively sharp acidity of a brut Champagne is too strong a contrast for most, except with some fresh fruit, light fruit tarts, *crème anglaise*, or floating island. Indeed, not-too-sweet fruit pies with a great dough and crust work fine. Avoid chocolate with Champagne, since its strong and beguiling flavors destroy the taste and finesse of even an average bubbly: it is that simple, and for people like me who are both chocolate and Champagne lovers it may seem tempting, but sometime, just sometime, one must follow a sensible rule. Maybe a fruity rosé Champagne has a fighting chance, but I have never found chocolate or Champagne showing their best when served together. And at today's price of Champagne . . . and chocolate, don't unnecessarily reduce the tasting and savoring experience. Now, if you have some Champagne left in a bottle or glass, it is a wonderful palate cleanser ten or twenty minutes later, and thereafter. Enjoy.

Finally, if you are still deciding whether or not to pop a cork with your meal, here's a little expression that may help. It is a favorite of some of the people who sell Champagne: "Burgundy makes us think of naughty things, Bordeaux makes us discuss them, and Champagne makes us do them." As I said, enjoy.

....

CHAPTER EIGHT

IN CASE YOU WERE ABOUT TO ASK

Read the Label

There was once an amusing American television commercial for a brand of spaghetti. It proclaimed it was the spaghetti harvesting season in Italy and showed a picturesque hillside of trees with spaghetti strands dangling from their many limbs. And if memory serves, there were peasants in centuries-old costumes, holding baskets, and filling them with freshly harvested pasta. Today we would call this artisanal pasta, or perhaps even "bio" or organic pasta, except, of course, for the fact that pasta does not grow on trees.

The humorous commercial played on the reality that most people neither connect what they eat, with what is in it, nor where it comes from. There is spaghetti and there is spaghetti, hundreds of brands plus homemade. There is, for example, whole wheat pasta that's touted today. Healthier? Less tasty? Pasta differences mostly have to do with the wheat that goes into the pasta, some of which are "enriched." What's that about? Do we need enriching? What are we putting into our bodies? But pasta is not a big offender loaded with added sugars or heavily salted or preserved with chemicals.

The list of common food items that have lost connection with their origins and genes is epidemic. I told the story in *French Women for All Seasons* of the boy who knew what apple pie was but not what an apple was. Just yesterday I was shopping in a gourmet specialty shop for fresh ricotta (now day-old homemade ricotta is a reason for a special detour), and I said to my husband, who was along for the walk, "Is there anything else we should get?" And he pointed to some dried sausages or *saucissons* as we call them in France, and said, "How about one or two of those?" (We occasionally nibble on a couple of slices while preparing dinner.) My response was to ask "How many times a week do you want to eat pork [the day before we had a pork roast]? Plus it is loaded with salt." A flash went off in his head and he said, "Gee [he really says gee], I know sausages are made from meat scraps and organs and body parts of animals we wouldn't eat if served on a plate, but I simply don't make a connection back to pigs—sausages are sausages." Yes, but unless they are labeled duck, venison, or turkey sausage or whatever, figure there's plenty of pork in them. It's implicit, but seemingly lost on the consumer.

I know reading labels: 1) is boring, 2) won't solve everything, 3) will scare you, but 4) is a lesson you will enjoy having learned, especially as it is a necessity in today's world of globalization with the ubiquitous availability of products created and "manufactured" far and wide, with new tastes regularly introduced from other cultures. I always look for two things as avoidance tips: 1) a long list of ingredients. I'd say five is fine—fifteen should set off alarms; and 2) corn syrup, high fructose corn syrup (yikes, an inexpensive sweetener and preservative that's low in nutritional value), words that sound like (and are) chemicals should be considered warnings. Plus I am alert to the quantity of salt and sugar contained in the labeled product. And let's recognize there are plenty of ambiguities on labels and ways for the food industry marketers both in the United States and abroad to mislead consumers.

Cereals and yogurts are two illustrative supermarket items that drive home the need to read labels and know what you are putting into your body. People with high blood pressure or water retention eat cereal without a clue that some are loaded with sodium. And they are sometimes eating cereal in order to lose weight to control their blood pressure and other health issues attributed to being overweight without knowing how much sugar and calories are in what they are eating. Almost the same thing can be said about yogurt.

A male friend of ours who was raised and lives outside the United States recently came to America to go to Canyon Ranch, a highly reputable spa, to lose weight, which also meant learning some things about nutrition for the first time. Over the years of busy life, busy travel, and busy entertainment he gained some pounds year after year. Then one day, as we say, he paid the price, which started with health issues that became more and more serious. He was told to lose weight and exercise but—you know the story. Finally he had reached the point when drugs, warnings, heart surgery, and the usual litany didn't work anymore, and it came to: you need to lose weight now, immediately, or you'll die soon. He needed help losing weight and regaining a healthy lifestyle and was able to afford the spa to start his "recovery."

When I saw him at a buffet brunch, I was not aware of the spa time but found him less heavy and, more important, looking different—let's say healthier and happier. So I said, "Wow," and congratulated him on the way he looked. He told me about his recent spa visit and how he had lost nine pounds (forty to go). He said he had learned a lot about nutrition, yet he was holding a bowl of cereal (looked like three portions to me—remember a cereal portion is ¾ cup, not 1½ or 2 cups). I couldn't help asking if this was the breakfast he had at the spa. More or less, he said, even though there he ate granola. After five minutes more of "eating" conversation, I learned he had trouble with water retention, so I did ask if he was aware of the salt content in cereal. He was not.

Without going into the brand—read a major and well-known cornflakes name—here is what I found on the label of a popular box of cornflakes: over fifteen ingredients, including three that worry me: salt, sugar, and high fructose corn syrup. Any idea why we would need sugar *plus* high fructose syrup, which is more sugar, in our cereal? And the best line on that box was the little label on top that said "Diabetes Friendly." Who are they kidding? (Does "diabetes friendly" mean it introduces you to diabetes? Or welcomes diabetics? I doubt the company caught the irony.) Well, lots of people don't read labels and don't know what they are eating. The sodium content in this cornflake box is 220 mg (milligrams) per serving (and what they classify as a serving is one ounce) and servings are commonly, I expect, exceeded in practice by a factor of two or even three. My husband's favorite cereal has less than half that amount of sodium per equivalent serving, and I eat an original pecan granola that has zero sodium in it.

Of course, you have to know what X mg of sodium means in the context of knowing what you are putting into your body and making informed decisions. The current recommended daily intake is between 500 mg minimum and 2,400 mg maximum, which in visual and equivalent terms is a quarter teaspoon of salt minimum and a teaspoon maximum. Think about that the next time you pick up a saltshaker. So what I am pointing out is many of us are mindlessly overdosing on salt. Diet soda? No calories, no cholesterol, but no salt? Wrong. The average diet soda has 28 mg of sodium. And, of course, since people think diet soda is free of most "bad" stuff, they drink not one but two and even three a day. And remember the sodium content of that bowl of cornflakes—before adding milk and more sodium?

People think yogurt is a wonder food, and it is, if it is plain yogurt. But go to a big supermarket in America, in Brazil, anywhere, including France, and as I have done with reporters, you can stand in front of a huge wall covered with dozens, even hundreds of types and brands of yogurt. Read the labels. Most do not make the cut for my idea of plain yogurt (yogurt is yogurt is yogurt, and the recipe calls for milk and culture, period; beware of the additives, calories, and the rest). The worst kinds list fifteen ingredients. Pleazzze. Make your own, it takes no time. All it takes is a quart of milk, the culture (you can buy it in a health food store or use a tablespoon of a plain—real—yogurt), bring to a near boil, add the culture, mix, put into the pots and *voilà*, the yogurt maker—just a warmer and jar container—will do the rest and you'll have a week of freshly made yogurt, six to eight containers depending on the "yogurt maker" you select (Cuisipro Donvier, Salton, and Euro Cuisine are good brands) for the price of *one*. If you top the yogurt with a little fresh fruit or some honey or wheat germ, you'll know what you are putting into it—and you.

Going to a spa is great if you can afford it (I know people who go once a year to shed the few pounds they've gained during that year, better than nothing but a form of yo-yo diet to me), but anyone can and should learn a bit about nutrition and practice label reading. Plus I hope they will pass their knowledge on to our younger generation to help fight the obesity epidemic and its consequences. Hopefully, nutrition will increasingly be taught in schools as well.

Water and Walking

Two cornerstones of my own diet are water and walking, and they merit a gentle reminder. Are eight 8-ounce glasses of water too much or not enough? It is sometimes difficult today to know what health advice to follow, since studies keep appearing that contradict past practices and wisdom and get their fifteen minutes of media attention only to be contradicted by new studies. When it comes to water, forget what you read, French women and most women know you cannot get enough water. And you don't just get it from a glass. Our bodies are 70 percent water; it makes sense that 70 percent of the food we eat should be high in water content. That's why mushrooms are a great diet food! Cucumbers, tomatoes, and melons are also high in water content.

Certainly drinking a large glass of water as I do each morning jump-starts our metabolism and rehydrates us after a dehydrating night of sleep. Water is good for our skin and hair. And water cuts our hunger and food cravings (with zero calories). It bears repeating that the next time you're hungry and feel like you need a snack during the middle of the day, try drinking a tall glass of water and see if the feeling subsides. Chances are, it will. Drinking water through the day should become automatic, and, if you can, a last glass before bedtime will complete the beneficial cycle.

Two other especially recommended times to drink your water are 30 minutes before and 90 minutes after meals. Bracketing meals with fluids helps you feel fuller for a longer period. But drinking a lot of water during meals slows down digestion and can distend the gastric pouch, which can result in discomfort.

A morning walk also kick-starts one's metabolism (some people use orange juice and coffee as morning stimulants), and moving well (regularity/consistency is key) before eating is as important to staying *bien dans sa peau* as eating well (balanced meals). They go together. As is notoriously known in most developed countries, a good third of the population doesn't move enough, and past age forty this increases risks for nasty conditions such as osteoporosis, atherosclerosis, high blood pressure, and, of course, more weight gain. Enough to give one more than a *frisson*. Not enough people know that all the organs of our body need to be involved to function properly and stay in good shape. (You've all heard the "use it or lose it" for memory and also lovemaking, but it's about the same for everything else.) Again, no need to go jogging for three hours a day, but a twenty- to thirty-minute daily walk and some other forms of movement of your choice two to three times a week for thirty to forty-five minutes will make a huge difference in your well-being.

To Detox or Not to Detox

So much has been and is currently being said about detox, but no one, including doctors, agrees on how important it is to consciously detox. If you are drinking enough water, you are enabling your body to flush out toxins (including vitamin and mineral overdoses, things that up to a point are good for you), as well as those that accumulate while you sleep. Or if you are lucky enough to get a massage, you are practicing detox. So, detoxing can be a pleasurable way of achieving balance. But what about all the products available out there from liquid fasts to herbal supplements and more? I'd agree that most are a scam.

My notion of detox is to flush out some toxins and give my body a little rest and reawaken my taste buds, which in turn will make me feel good and help reduce the amount I eat without much effort.

What works for me and worked for my mother and grandmother is the Magical Leek Broth 36-hour detox. So does a soup day or simply a light food day. In my book that does not mean artificially reduced low-calorie "light" foods, but whole foods in small portions, limited amounts of fresh and well-selected food high in fiber, omega-3, and all the good things we need. I like a few prunes and yogurt with half a piece of toasted seven-grain bread, a soup and/or salad with some veggies and lemon vinaigrette versus oil, and fruit on a relatively light food day. Detox does not mean deprivation or starvation; it should not last more than a few days and can be as short as a day. The best short detox is a day of ever so lightly salted vegetable soups or bouillons for lunch and dinner.

My friend Nicole likes to do a three- to five-day light meal detox after the holiday season or at the end of winter. Her breakfast is lemon juice with lukewarm water followed with fruit salad or compote and a cup of green tea. For lunch: 3 ounces of canned tuna in olive oil with fennel, tomatoes, and olives, and ⅓ cup of whole grain brown rice. For dinner: soup and fruit compote. The last two days she adds 3 ounces of fish or white chicken meat or tofu. She claims that after this, she feels reborn.

Our complex body knows how to manage excesses, but in the twenty-first century, excesses tend to be too often and too extreme for many people. We do, after all, absorb all kinds of chemicals through food, air, and water, so a short detox can't hurt. Listen to and watch your body.

I also like to think of my kind of detox as an easy, fast, and yummy way to a 3/5/7-pound loss in 3/5/7 days. In addition to the leek broth jump-start, when I want to shed a few pounds, I follow a Magical Breakfast Cream detox scenario for three days to a week. (It is important to stick to the basic yogurt/flaxseed oil/lemon juice *Tante* Berthe recipe, see page 15.) It is a nice and delicious way to reset one's body and take a break. The weight loss is more a side effect than a goal, unless you use it to change your relationship with food so that you do not return to the eating pattern that put the weight on in the first place. No yo-yo. A periodic recalibration, yes. Again, don't think about extending this beyond a few days or a week. Think about a quarterly refresher.

For three mornings in a row, I have the MBC and coffee for breakfast. For lunch and dinner, I eat steamed vegetables plus fish or white meat chicken for protein. And I cut out bread and wine for three days or more. (Or, say, cakes, cookies, and pastries if they are your offenders.) Try it, a lot of people felt better, shed a few pounds, did not feel hungry, gave their body all the necessary nutrients, and came back with added energy, well-being, and differences in skin, hair, mood, and much more after three to five days.

My Husband Eats Like a Pig!

I've borrowed the words of Brillat-Savarin many times that you are what you eat. If you are surrounded by a husband or a family that guzzles down junk and rushes through dinner without the simplest care or respect for the food and the meal, even the strongest-willed French lady would become frustrated and frequently fall off track.

"My husband eats like a pig" is a complaint I've read and heard many times. One woman wrote to me that she was fed up with her husband inhaling his dinner in less than five minutes and was concerned for her sons, who were following in his bad example, wolfing down their food like there was no tomorrow. I immediately felt sorry for her. That was no way to "enjoy" dinner: night after night of being left at the table to finish her dinner alone, the men in her life polishing off their food before she even had a chance to sit down. Sound familiar? I even heard complaints about children and husbands who refused to eat new, better quality food being presented, opting instead for frozen TV dinners and junk food without a single "thank you" to the budding new chef (aka Mom) in the kitchen. And it doesn't stop there. I've been questioned continuously by women wanting to know how to overcome food obstacles between them and their spouses, boyfriends, stubborn relatives, and children. Many women feel that they cannot live the French lifestyle without the cooperation of their spouses and family. And I understand their frustration, but where there's a will, there's a way. After all, we French women can be stubborn, too.

Teach Them a Lesson

"My big kid of a hubby grew up on junk and a fridge filled with soda available any time. He still comes home from work many nights with a Coke can in his hand and a candy bar before dinner!" Alice vented on my website's message board.

A candy bar *and* soda before dinner? You've got to be kidding. Could Alice's husband really be that reckless and irresponsible about his health? Maybe not. In my experience, most men are often unaware of what they are putting into their bodies. Ditto for children. They don't cook. They don't read ingredients, and, even if they did, they usually don't have a frame of reference for what is healthy versus unhealthy, a proper portion size, or nutritional data. I am singing an old song in a new verse. If you want to coax them into eating better, you must make them understand what they are putting into their bodies (and what it does once inside). Take Joyce, a fwdgf.com member who shared her story about a friend who taught her children a life-changing math problem.

"A friend tried to cajole, rant, and nag her children into cutting their soda addiction. Though she never kept it in the house, they'd buy it at school, or drink it at friends' houses. What finally did work was a little math problem and science experiment. She had them help her calculate how much sugar (in teaspoons) is in a typical can of soda. Then she had them measure out the teaspoons into a clean glass and fill the glass with 12 ounces of water from a soda can. 'Now drink it,' she said. The kids were horrified and refused to drink it! They considerably cut their soda consumption when they were able to see what they were really drinking. Her words meant nothing to her teens, but the reality was hard to ignore!"

Fantastique idea, I must admit. Try it with your own soda addicts. And if your husband or teenagers still don't want to listen to reason, try Michelle's solution, who told me she demanded her husband keep his twelve-packs of soda, Ding Dongs, and other poison snacks in his car after he refused to stop bringing them in the house! Hey, if you can't convey the harm he's doing to his own body, at least you can keep the junk out of sight of you and your children. Don't be afraid to put your foot down like Michelle; this is your family's health you're talking about!

Peu à Peu . . . and Patience

Let's face it, men are creatures of habit, and one of the hardest things to break is a bad habit. Chances are your husband comes from a long history of unhealthy, old-fashioned American-style eating. As Cathy said, "My husband grew up with very bland, oversalted frozen food, and beef nightly. No fresh anything, nothing even remotely different or tasty." So how do you get them to step out of the frozen food box, and into the French lifestyle? Remember, *peu à peu*. (If I say it three times it is true!) You must introduce new and different things little by little. Almost every woman who has had success with a stubborn family or husband has given the same advice. Fwdgf.com members Jan and Lisa suggest, "Offer a 'weird' thing with more familiar things. I insist everyone take two bites' worth of everything made. My teens are often surprised that they like something new," and "My best suggestion is to start small—the resistance is already built, so go slow. Start by adding an extra veggie to your regular recipes, weaning them off white bread, adding in whole grains, explaining gently every day how health and foods are important. You'll get there!"

In *French Women Don't Get Fat*, I wrote about learning to spot your personal offenders. But what if eating with your husband or significant other *is* an offender? Marcy realized it was one of hers: "If there is an offender, it is eating with my husband. Not only do we differ greatly when it comes to eating healthy but when we do eat together, I feel as if I'm galloping away trying to catch up with him. I don't know if he even chews his food, but our dinner is usually a stressful event for me."

And I can't tell you how many times I've heard women say that by the time their husbands and children are finished with dinner, they've barely touched their salad. Cope by telling your family that even after they've finished their dinner, you'd like them to stay at the table until everyone is done. Lead by example, pausing to put down your fork while asking family members a question about their day. Little by little you may see the pace of your meals start to slow down.

Next, subtly change the way you and/or your family thinks about the dinner itself. Dinner can be an aesthetic event, not just a forum for refueling. Elevate the experience of your meals with a tablecloth, nice plates, and a presentation that makes your family say, "Wow!" Little touches such as chopped parsley or a dollop of crème fraîche in a bowl of soup can transform a boring dish into a conversation piece. Malcolm Gladwell noted in *The Tipping Point* that the most effective way to reduce street crime in a community is to change the appearance of the neighborhood. The same principle applies here: change the appearance, change the entire mind-set. Sometimes big changes require only small initiatives. This is a bit like the art of seduction. Eating well can be lovely—from biting into really fresh fruit, to the time it takes to make a delicious salad, to learning how to roast a chicken properly, to buying really good Parmigiano-Reggiano. It's yummy.

When it comes specifically to husbands, try to explain to them your reasoning. One reader suggested, "When I am embracing a new idea/lifestyle/mind-set, I talk with my hubby about it, sharing my enthusiasm. I try not to insist that he copy me, just listen to my ideas and energy. Inevitably he starts buying into it along the way."

And if he really won't listen? Be stubborn, stay on the course you've charted for yourself. In fact, the same woman who complained "my husband eats like a pig" applied this very principle. "I used to get caught in eating and drinking faster, just to keep up and get my share! No longer! I use their eating habits to my advantage. While they're on their second or third helping of a dish, I can still be grazing on my first. There is no temptation for a snip of seconds when the food is already gone! Dinner is not a competitive sport!"

Men's Health, Women's Health, Children's Health

Have you and your husband, boyfriend, brother, or male friend ever dieted together, only to find that he was outpacing you in the weight-loss race, despite the fact that you were eating the same thing? (You may have even been eating less.) Men have more natural muscle mass than women. Since the number of calories you burn is proportionate to the amount of muscle you have, men naturally burn more calories than women, even when eating the same foods, similar portions, and exercising together. So the next time you succumb to sharing that Twinkie with your hubby, remember he's going to burn it off much quicker than you. It's a harsh reality: Women cannot eat, and in some ways cook, like men.

But there's another reason to get your husband and children involved in the French lifestyle, beyond just wanting to stay within the confines of your own new meal plans: their health.

Women tend to gain weight in their hips and behinds; men are more likely to put on weight around the waist. Doctors are not sure why, but the risk factors of developing heart disease and other complications such as high blood pressure, diabetes, sleep apnea, and even cancer increase dramatically in those who store fat around their waists, especially those with a waist size over forty inches. So, those few extra inches on his waistline may be more harmful than you think. Thankfully, men tend to lose weight rather quickly when they cut out their offenders (we women are not as lucky in this department!). After a couple weeks of the new French lifestyle in her home, an ecstatic member commented about her husband, "He didn't really need to lose weight, but he'd been concerned about his little belly that showed up in his early forties. It's now gone!"

As for children, it's vital to get them started on the right track as early as possible: lifetime eating habits begin at a very young age. The USDA has reported that only 36 percent of United States children eat the recommended three to five servings of daily vegetables, and only 26 percent eat the two to four recommended servings of fruit. These numbers are abysmal. Many mothers have complained that they receive major resistance from their kids on eating healthy food. But for little kids, there should be no choice. You do the food shopping, you make the rules. Feel free to get creative, too. If your child has an insatiable sweet tooth, learn to reframe their notion of dessert as did Monica, a very resourceful woman, who turned her kids' obsession with ice cream sundaes into a healthy fix by creating a yogurt parfait station in the kitchen after dinner. She realized a small bowl of yogurt and a station of healthy toppings such as granola, chopped fruits, and honey gave her children the illusion they were indulging in a decadent treat. Other mothers have found that fresh fruit over a little ice cream instead of packaged cookies and candy was happily accepted by their children. Be realistic, though, do not strive for perfection. They will always find junk at a friend's house, or find something to complain about. Do try to instill awareness and a few values in them for what they are putting into their body, and help cultivate a taste for fruits and veggies.

Head to the Kitchen

The lack of connection to food and cooking is what prevents many of us from finding balance, harmony, and pleasure. Of all the reader mail/email I have received over the years, those who reported the most success with changing to the healthy holistic lifestyle I describe in my writings are the ones who started to cook or cooked more, or more often. Makes sense to me. Cooking means connection and is a key to changing your relationship with food and pleasure, and until you understand and control what you are putting in your body, you are merely following a plan without a master: you.

Each of us is responsible for our own body. And it all starts with respect for one's body, as we only have one, right? Respect may not always mean love, but if one respects one's body, that respect surely will grow into taming it, then loving it, and once you love it, you'll take care of it and be responsible for it. Common sense. It's the basic story of the little prince and the fox about making friends. Changing your relationship with food means just that. Make food (and your body) not your enemy but your friend and head for the kitchen instead of the television set or whatever else you pick to do to avoid cooking.

It goes without saying that homemade food, where one can control fat, salt, and sugar, helps us lose weight or at least control our weight. Plus, let's be honest: today with all the gadgets to help us cook, making a meal is not such a big deal. In many cases, it takes just a bit longer than getting canned or prepared food ready. So, *pas d'excuses*. A bit of planning and organizing and soon one can learn to make dinner in 20 to 30 minutes daily.

Globalization has its side effects in both cooking and the kitchen. Today, in France, depending which statistics one reads, over 60 percent of people in their twenties have no culinary knowledge. Starting from scratch, we must teach them (they usually start panicking when they have kids to feed) how to shop at the market (including recognizing products) so they can pick the right products and ways of cooking vegetables in a simple, quick, and flavorful way following the seasons. Many people are getting tired of poor eating (read prepared dishes and fast food), and cooking classes are growing like mushrooms. This is something totally new in France, where nine out of ten French people have never taken a cooking class. Now it's more like a hobby and gone are the long, expensive and complicated ones.

Today, one of the most successful cooking courses/programs in France is L'atelier des Chefs, created by two young men passionate about cooking. The key word is casual and their classes are short—one hour. Their principle during lunchtime is cooking for thirty minutes and then eating lunch—fun, inexpensive, and a way to be with people (not a small aspect at a time where so many tech gadgets isolate human beings in many ways). What one learns is to make one dish per class, an ideal way for most "students" who have zero knowledge. In hard economic times, what these students learn is that home cooking not only means better quality (less salt, sugar, and fat) but also huge savings, as it's not that difficult to prepare a meal for a family of four. The key is to go to schools linked with real chefs, since some are managed by amateurs who are not automatically feeding people's needs, let alone have the appropriate knowledge. People need a basic savoir faire, tips and tricks, and what chefs call *le bon geste* (the right technique). People need reassurance that they can go home and duplicate the meal, and in a relaxed environment everyone comes out with self-confidence. The proof is men are discovering that women love men who know how to cook, so it's time to change the famous French saying *l'amour de l'homme passe par l'estomac.* With a few classes and good basics, it's then easy to go home and practice and make one's own innovations and improvisations soon enough.

The French Call It *BIO* . . .
Eating Organic

I get asked a lot about my take on organic foods. Not all organic food is automatically of the greatest quality, and, as far as nutrients are concerned, there's not much difference between most organic foods and their nonorganic commercial counterparts. If you buy most of your food locally and seasonally, and minimize processed foods in your diet, you are already doing well.

When I can, however, I eat organic produce for two reasons. The first is taste. Most of the organic food I buy at the Greenmarket tastes a lot better than what I find in supermarkets. Part of that is the little extra concentration and purity of flavor I find in organic produce, but I suspect an added flavor booster is the freshness of Greenmarket produce over supermarket produce. Many but not all organic foods from a Greenmarket taste better to me than organic items from a supermarket, and I attribute that to relative freshness more than the particular origin and cultivation of the food. In terms of price, yes, organic is a bit more expensive (think about all the additional cultivation work required, the lower yields, and other "uncommercial" practices and be thankful there are people who care to raise these foods to feed us), but remember taste first. Here my theory of "it's all in the first few bites" applies, so I buy a bit less, enjoy it more, and it works out affordably and healthily.

The second reason I prefer organic is more important. I prefer eating food raised without pesticides, chemical fertilizers, and supplements. I don't want to put those things in my body with any regularity. The potential for side effects such as allergies and diseases these chemicals cause is more than I want to risk. There are certain items such as eggs and chickens—you've all heard about those zillion chickens that never see the light, look anorexic, are fed garbage and pills, taste artificial, and literally produce "rotten" eggs. I would rather not eat them. Amen.

Dans ma cuisine or In My Kitchen

Alors, if cooking with fresh, high-quality ingredients is the most important part of making a good meal (it is), then having a kitchen stocked with the right staples, spices, and tools to pull it all together is the second most important. Many people find it tricky to keep a well-stocked pantry, but knowing which spices to have on hand and which kitchen tools to invest in is actually quite simple—and can save you money in the long run. (And learn that dried parsley, basil, and a few other spices are a waste of money—their flavors are real and explosive only when fresh, so buy or grow them fresh.) I own a wok and a *tajine,* but I never use them. They were given to me as gifts. I eat Chinese and Middle Eastern cuisine, but don't make it at home. That's not me. I cook French, Italian, Mediterranean, and American. I cook food that reflects my travels and experiences, the recipes and tips I've picked up from friends and family along the way. So, what follows is what I have in my kitchen based on what I like to eat, and what will more than cover what is needed for the recipes in this book.

DANS LES PLACARDS OR IN THE PANTRY

Anchovies (canned)	Dried fruits (golden raisins, cranberries)
Baking powder	Flour
Baking soda	Garlic
Beans	Honey
Capers	Mustard (Dijon or grainy)
Dark chocolate (does not stay prime for long)	Nuts (walnuts, almonds particularly)
	Oatmeal/rolled oats

Oil (olive, safflower, walnut, vegetable)

Onions

Pasta (spaghetti, linguine, ziti, farfalle)

Peanut butter

Potatoes

Quinoa

Red wine, sherry, and balsamic vinegar

Rice (brown, basmati)

Sardines (canned)

Shallots

Spirits (Pernod, Calvados)

Sugar (brown and white)

Tomatoes (canned)

Tomato paste

Tuna (canned in oil or water)

Vanilla beans and/or premium pure vanilla extract

Whole wheat pasta

DANS LE FRIGO OR IN THE FRIDGE

Bacon

Butter (unsalted)

Carrots

Celery

Champagne

Cheese (Parmesan, pecorino, goat cheese, and a semi-hard cow's cheese)

Cornichons

Crème fraîche

Dry white wine or vermouth

Eggs

Fennel

Fresh herbs (parsley, basil, rosemary, thyme—or in a window box)

Fromage blanc

Jam (once opened)

Leeks

Lemons

Maple syrup (once opened)

Milk, 2%

Mustard (grainy and/or Dijon once opened)

Olives (black and green)

Onions

Oranges

Prunes (once opened)

Yogurt

DANS LE CONGÉLATEUR OR IN THE FREEZER

Blueberries

Bread

Chicken, skinless and boneless breasts

Chicken and beef stock, frozen in 1- to
2-cup servings

Edamame

Peas

Pesto (pesto freezes very nicely—I like
to store mine in ice cube–size servings)

Puff pastry

Raspberries

ÉPICES OR SPICES

Cardamom

Cayenne pepper

Cinnamon

Cumin

Curry powder

Nutmeg

Paprika or piment d'Espelette

Pepper, black

Peppercorns

Red pepper flakes

Salt (kosher, sea, and fleur de sel)

Star anise

Tarragon

SUR LE COMPTOIR OR ON THE COUNTERTOP

Bowl for fruits and vegetables that
should not be refrigerated (tomatoes,
peaches, bananas)

Coffee maker

Salt and pepper grinder

Slotted spoon, spatulas, whisks in a
ceramic container

Small food processor

Teakettle

Toaster

BATTERIE DE CUISINE OR COOKING EQUIPMENT

I've omitted the tools that every kitchen must have: a pot with a tight-fitting lid, at least two or three sharp, high-quality knives for cutting meat and produce, a skillet or sauté pan, and oven-safe dishes for baking. Once you've invested in these, you can move on to the following:

Apple corer	*Nonstick baking mat*
Baking sheet	*Offset spatula/fish spatula*
Blender	*Parchment paper*
Cheese grater	*Ring molds*
Colander	*Scale (electronic or mechanical)*
Double boiler	*Springform pan*
Food mill	*Stand mixer*
Knife sharpener/stone	*Steamer insert*
Lemon reamer	*Tongs*
Mandoline (the inexpensive one)	*Vegetable peeler*
Measuring cups and spoons	*Wine corkscrew*
Meat thermometer	*Zester*

AU MARCHÉ OR AT THE MARKET

Now that you've stocked your kitchen with every French woman's and chef's essentials, it's off to the market for the really important stuff: fresh, local produce. Of course, you'll have to tailor your list to the time of year, as seasonality is still the guiding force of the French palate. With the staples I mentioned and a few of the suggestions here, you will have a balanced meal.

SPRING/SUMMER	*Corn*
Apricots	*Eggplant*
Artichokes	*Fava beans*
Asparagus	*Meyer lemons*
Berries	*Peas*

Ramps
Rhubarb
Spinach
Tomatoes

FALL/WINTER
Apples
Broccoli
Mushrooms (locally foraged)
Pears
Pumpkin
Quince
Squash varieties (heirloom)

AVAILABLE YEAR-ROUND
Bananas
Citrus
Cucumbers
Endives
Garlic
Grapes
Kiwi
Onions
Potatoes
Root vegetables (carrots, parsnips, turnips)
Salad greens
Shallots
Zucchini

IN CASE YOU WERE ABOUT TO ASK

CUISINER DANS LA CUISINE,
OR COOKING IN THE KITCHEN

*I*n the end, this is a cookbook, after all; this is a recipe book. So, head to the kitchen and cook a few things. It is the best way to understand what you put into your body and is an act filled with pleasures. With due appreciation for the ambiguity and caginess of generalizations, I conclude by observing that:

- Cooking is an *act of love,* for sure, as those of us who've cooked all our lives know that to spoil others is a great source of pleasure, even though for some who cook dinner every night it may sometimes seem like a chore.

- Cooking is *self-expression,* a way of finding the aromas, colors, and flavors that define your personality.

- Cooking is *nourishment* of the body and soul.

- Cooking is *sensibility:* think about the art of making a sauce no matter how simple.

- Cooking is a *contemplative* experience reaching and probing deep in our thoughts and emotions.

- Cooking is *seduction*, from creating the atmosphere and setting, to the giving of what is loved and shared, to the cumulative engagement of the senses and being.

- Cooking is *memory*, as it links to a person's culture and values. Whenever we eat something, the taste and memory of all the times we have eaten that dish live in the present.

- Cooking is *conviviality* and *sharing*, especially when cooking with others—a spouse, a friend, or children.

- Cooking is *fun*, from picking the produce to preparing the dishes to serving the final preparation, and sharing the results with others.

- Cooking is *relaxing*, and focusing on your preparation can be a getaway from daily stress.

- Cooking is *sexy*—like a kiss, a physical emotion, a union between human beings, and an experience that is sensual, engaging all of one's senses.

- Cooking is *le goût* or *taste*, a heightening awareness and refinement of the senses in conflict, in harmony, and in combination and celebration with one another.

- Cooking is *improvisational;* recipes are a guide not a formula for intimidation. Make do with what you have and how you like it.

- Cooking is good for the mind, *good for mental health*, using your hands to craft a delicious and complete finished dish or meal.

- Cooking is *conversation*, as a meal gathers values, tastes, rituals, and words that are passed on for generations and play an extremely important social role not only over holiday seasons.

- Cooking is *respecting the seasons* and appreciating the fleeting moment of the short availability of cherries, apricots, asparagus, clementines, and much more.

- Cooking is *time:* like writing, it demands that impalpable seasoning. It takes time, but then time is something we can control. It is an investment, a brilliant use of time to feed and nurture ourselves and those we care about.

- Cooking is *reading* from a recipe in a cookbook or on the Internet, thus absorption *and learning.*

- Cooking is an *art form* and obliges us to be creative while involving smelling, touching, tasting, savoring at a given time and place and then it's gone, until the next time.

- Cooking is *humor*—let us not take ourselves seriously and make dishes with thirty ingredients, a *batterie de cuisine* with two days of preparation. If a chicken falls off the counter, pick it up; if the cake cracks, frost it.

- Cooking is a *social act* that reveals ourselves, our attitudes and behaviors, and telltale characteristics.

- Cooking is *education* and eating at the table is a good way to teach kids about respecting food, learning to be responsible for their own bodies, and teaching them the art of conversation, manners, and pleasure.

- Cooking is *transportive.* It helps us relive our childhoods through favorite foods and people, say Grandma's coffee cake, and brings us to places where we've eaten memorable dishes, perhaps a pastry in Paris or a grilled fish along a lake.

- Cooking is *playing jazz;* one can never cook the same dish twice or have the same experience or pleasure.

- Cooking is both *finite* and *infinite* along life's continuum.

- Cooking is *pleasure* and an integral part of what is called *l'équilibre alimentaire,* a *balanced* approach to eating.

- Cooking is the *reward* for shopping.

- Cooking is *healthy*.

- Cooking is *slimming*.

REMERCIEMENTS

Once upon a time I was cooking lunch for a journalist who was interviewing me for a women's magazine. As I was about to put the main-course fish in the oven, the oven seemingly died. After an attempt to restart it, I realized I was out of my depth and quickly switched to a stovetop preparation, talking the entire time to the journalist, who was busily taking notes. Stuff happens. I took it in stride, but the journalist was impressed and published the story of the snafu and saving grace. I thank her and all of my guests in America and France who have good-naturedly eaten my food. Sometimes it wasn't up to my standards and sometimes it wasn't up to their tastes, but this book is a result of what I learned. Generally, things worked out fine.

Several people stand out as noble contributors in their roles of testers, testees, and collaborators in support of this book: my mother, though no longer with me save in spirit, certainly gave me my love for food and good cooking, and prepared for me many of the dishes included here. My husband, Edward, has eaten all of the dishes in this cookbook; indeed, sometimes three days in a row as I played with the recipe. He maintained his sense of humor and weight throughout. He is very much part of the story told in these pages.

Erin Jones once again provided me with valuable help with a manuscript and in this case with some additional recipe testing and research. Sarah Hearn used her substantial food and cooking expertise to make this a stronger offering, including by retesting the recipes for taste, proportions, and consistency in the Boston air and on her apartment stove. I welcome and appreciate Erin and Sarah's contributions, which more than saved me from a fallen soufflé or two. Similarly, I thank a long list of French and primarily Provence friends who shared and fussed over recipes with me over the years.

My editor, Peter Borland, has as a result of our continuing collaboration acquired an early addiction to MBC (Magical Breakfast Cream), and with this effort has notched his first cookbook during a distinguished career as an editor. Once again, it was an easy and rewarding experience working with Peter, who in many ways made this a better book than I was capable of doing on my own. Thanks also go to Judith Curr and the entire Atria team of publishing professionals for their support, enthusiasm, and expertise.

In one of those pleasant surprises in life, it seems I have acquired an official MG illustrator. My friend R. "Nick" Nichols has again used his wit and wondrous powers for illustration to make my prosaic efforts attractive beyond my imagination. Thank you. I hope readers appreciate your talent as much as I do.

My agent, Kathy Robbins, has been a major collaborator and conspirator throughout my encore career as an "author." Without her, there would be no *French Women Don't Get Fat* to follow up with this cookbook. And without her and Rachelle Bergstein from The Robbins Office reading and worrying about this book, it would be a vastly inferior effort. It's great to have the entire Robbins Office behind what I have done and do.

I recognize I am blessed with such a consistent and gifted team of people noted here as well as a few other guest members along the way. I appreciate that daily. But I am most blessed with readers who encouraged me to write this and my other books and whose lives touch mine in so many ways. Thank you, dear readers. *Merci.* Now do go and cook something.

INDEX

"Aïoli," Quick, 140

almonds:

Haricots Verts Salad with Peaches and Almonds, 78

Quinoa with Almonds, Hazelnuts, and Apricots, 33

Yogurt and Nut "Cocktail," 197

anchovies:

Fusilli with Spinach and Anchovies, 87

Ricotta and Anchovy *Tartines*, 39

apples:

Apple Compote with Pistachios, 184

Avocado-Apple Salad with Gambas, 227

Baked Apples with Lemon Cream, 253

Cheese-Apple Mille-Feuille, 50

Grandma Louise's Oatmeal with Grated Apple, 214

Grated Fruit and Veggie "Slaw," 76

Italian-style Fennel and Apple Salad, 75

Onion *Poêlée* with Apples, 173

Pork Chops with Apples, 145

Pumpkin and Apple Gratin, 167

Pumpkin and Apple Soup, 117

Sweet *Flammekueche*, 54–55

apricots:

Apricot Tart, 232–33

Quinoa with Almonds, Hazelnuts, and Apricots, 33

arugula, Spaghetti with Lime and Arugula, 89

asparagus:

Asparagus with Yogurt Dressing, 79

Salmon with Leeks and Asparagus *en Papillote*, 162–63

avocado:

Avocado-Apple Salad with Gambas, 227

Crab *Tartines* Avocado, 240

Endive and Avocado Gazpacho, 65

Grapefruit, Avocado, and Caviar Mille-Feuille, 47

bacon, Scrambled Eggs with Herbs and Smoked Salmon–Bacon Toast, 239

balance, 63

bananas:

Peanut Butter Banana Oatmeal, 31

Raspberry-Banana Smoothie, 189

Strawberry-Banana Oatmeal Smoothie, 32

beans:

Black Olive Potato Salad with Fava Beans, 135

Haricots Verts Salad with Peaches and Almonds, 78

Quinoa with Peas and Favas, 127

Velouté of Haricots Verts with Peppers and Ham, 220

beef, Stuffed Zucchini, 252

beets:

Beet and Ginger Gazpacho, 66

Beet and Zucchini Gazpacho, 67

Mâche, Celeriac, and Beet Salad, 72

Quinoa and Beet Salad, 134

Black Olive Potato Salad with Fava Beans, 135

blue cheese:

Cream of Celeriac with Pear and Blue Cheese, 118

Endives *Confites* with Blue Cheese Crostini, 172

Fromage Blanc with Blue Cheese and Chives, 51

Pear and Blue Cheese *Tartines*, 42

Bollinger, Lily, 14

Bouillabaisse Twenty-first Century, 96–97

breakfast, 7–34

author's notes on, 9–14

comfort food, 29–34

eggs, 20–28

Magical Breakfast Cream, 11–19

Brillat-Savarin, Anthelme, 270

broccoli rabe, Orecchiette with Broccoli Rabe and Sausage, 119

brunch, 35–57

author's notes on, 35–36

brunch (*cont.*)
  special and luxurious, 45–57
  tartines, 36–44
Brunch for 4 or 8, 238–40
  Crab Tartines Avocado, 240
  menu, 238
  Scrambled Eggs with Herbs and
    Smoked Salmon–Bacon
    Toast, 239
Bruschetta with Escarole, 221
Budwig, Johanna, 14
Butternut Squash Soup, 114

calories, cutting, 63
capers:
  John Dory with Tomatoes and
    Capers, 100
  Roasted Cauliflower with Raisins
    and Capers, 170
Caramelized Chicken with
  Vegetable "Pancake," 104–5
Caramelized Endives, 169
cardamom, (Eggless) Chocolate
  Mousse with Cardamom, 203
carrots:
  Carrot and Celeriac Salad, 73
  Carrot and Orange Soup, 215
  Carrot Parsnip Purée, 174
  Carrot Soup with Yogurt and
    Kiwi, 70
  Grated Fruit and Veggie "Slaw,"
    76
  Mackerel with Carrots and
    Leeks, 137
  Potage d'Hiver (Winter Soup),
    115
  Roasted Carrots and Pumpkin
    with Herbs, 130
  Roasted Vegetables with Cumin,
    166
  Sardines with Carrots and Leeks,
    136
  Sweet-and-Sour Carrot Salad,
    177
cauliflower:
  Cauliflower Purée, 128
  Roasted Cauliflower with Raisins
    and Capers, 170

caviar:
  Croque Monsieur Eric Ripert
    Style, 56
  Grapefruit, Avocado, and Caviar
    Mille-Feuille, 47
celeriac:
  Carrot and Celeriac Salad, 73
  Cream of Celeriac with Pear and
    Blue Cheese, 118
  Grated Fruit and Veggie "Slaw,"
    76
  Lentil and Celeriac Soup, 116
  Mâche, Celeriac, and Beet Salad,
    72
  Sea Bass with Celeriac-Mint
    Salsa, 95
Champagne, 241–61
  author's notes on, 243–48,
    259–61
  Champagne Medley Dinner,
    254–58
  Chicken *au Champagne*, 251
  Chicken *Tout au Champagne*
    Menu, 249–53
  opening the bottle, 246–48
  types and styles, 245–46
Champagne Medley Dinner,
  254–58
  Duck Breasts with Pears, 257
  menu, 254
  Prosciutto Wrapped Around
    Grissini, 255
  Scallops *Maison Blanche,* 256
  Strawberry Parfait, 258
cheese:
  Cheese-Apple Mille-Feuille, 50
  Clafoutis Provençal, 46
  Cream of Celeriac with Pear and
    Blue Cheese, 118
  Cucumber, Prosciutto, and
    Parmesan *Tartines,* 40
  Endives *Confites* with Blue
    Cheese Crostini, 172
  Fromage Blanc with Blue Cheese
    and Chives, 51
  Goat Cheese and Hazelnut
    Tartines, 38
  Leeks and Onion Parmesan, 222

Leeks Mozzarella, 133
Lemon Ricotta Pancakes, 226
Macaroni with Ricotta and
  Walnuts, 124
Parmesan Polenta with
  Prosciutto, 44
Pear and Blue Cheese *Tartines,* 42
Provençal Omelet, 23
Ricotta and Anchovy *Tartines,* 39
Scallop "Ceviche" with Mango
  and Parmesan, 230
Spaghetti Carbonara, 120–21
Spaghetti Carbonara *alla*
  Edoardo, 122–23
Zucchini and Fresh Goat Cheese
  Frittata, 28
chicken:
  Caramelized Chicken with
    Vegetable "Pancake," 104–5
  Carefree Chicken, 150
  Chicken *au Champagne*, 251
  Chicken en Croûte Fiona Style,
    147
  Chicken *à la Tunisienne,* 149
  Chicken with Spinach *en*
    Papillote, 103
  Curried Chicken with
    Cucumber, 106
  Italian-style Chicken, 148
  Roasted Chicken with Endives,
    217–18
Chicken *Tout au Champagne* Menu,
  249–53
  Baked Apples with Lemon
    Cream, 253
  Chicken *au Champagne*, 251
  menu, 249
  Poêlée of Mushrooms, 250
  Stuffed Zucchini, 252
chocolate:
  Chocolate-Coffee Verrines, 193
  Classic Chocolate Mousse,
    236–37
  (Eggless) Chocolate Mousse with
    Cardamom, 203
  Madeleines *au Chocolat,* 204–5
  Pineapple, Yogurt, and
    Chocolate Verrines, 192

Spiced Chocolate Mousse, 206
Tarte au Chocolat, 224
Yogurt with *Crème Chocolat,* 229
Clafoutis Provençal, 46
closures, 179–206
    Apple Compote with Pistachios, 184
    Apricot Tart, 232–33
    author's notes on, 181–83, 211
    Baked Apples with Lemon Cream, 253
    chocolate, 203–6, 224, 229, 236–37
    Crêpes, 194–95
    Fruit Salad with Quinoa, 186
    Lemon Curd, 202
    Panna Cotta, 200–201
    Pear and Date au Gratin, 185
    smoothies and verrines, 187–94
    Strawberry Parfait, 258
    yogurt dishes, 197–99, 229, 258
Cod with Fennel and Orange *en Papillote,* 159
comfort food, 29–34
    author's notes on, 29
    Cream of Wheat with Cranberries and Walnuts, 34
    Grandma Louise's Oatmeal with Grated Apple, 214
    Oatmeal with Lemon Zest and Prunes, 30
    Peanut Butter Banana Oatmeal, 31
    Quinoa with Almonds, Hazelnuts, and Apricots, 33
    Strawberry-Banana Oatmeal Smoothie, 32
cooking:
    author's notes on, 285–88
    and globalization, 277
    homemade food, 276–78
    ingredients, 279–83
Crab *Tartines* Avocado, 240
cranberries, Cream of Wheat with Cranberries and Walnuts, 34
Cream of Celeriac with Pear and Blue Cheese, 118
Cream of Wheat with Cranberries and Walnuts, 34

Crêpes, 194–95
Crimini Salad, 82
Croque Monsieur Eric Ripert Style, 56
cucumber:
    Cucumber, Prosciutto, and Parmesan *Tartines,* 40
    Curried Chicken with Cucumber, 106
cumin:
    Roasted Vegetables with Cumin, 166
    Tilapia with Cumin and Mushrooms, 94
curry:
    Curried Chicken with Cucumber, 106
    Eggplant with Curry and Honey, 171
    Mackerel with Curry and Leeks, 141
    Vegetable Curry, 165

dates, Pear and Date au Gratin, 185
daurade, Roasted *Daurade* (Sea Bream) with Vegetables, 223
desserts, *see* closures
detox, 269–70
    Magical Leek Broth, 68–69
dinner *à table,* 107–50
    author's notes on, 109–13
    fish, 136–44
    meat dishes, 145–50
    pasta, 119–25
    soups, 114–18
    vegetables, 126–35
Duck Breasts *à la Gasconne* with Wild Rice, 235
Duck Breasts with Pears, 257

eggplant:
    Clafoutis Provençal, 46
    Eggplant with Curry and Honey, 171
    Penne with Eggplant and Tuna, 84
    Ratatouille, 80–81
    Vegetable Curry, 165

eggs, 20–28
    author's notes on, 20–21
    Clafoutis Provençal, 46
    Fried Eggs, Spanish Style, 25
    Ham and Leek Frittata, 27
    Poached Eggs with Salmon and Spinach, 26
    Provençal Omelet, 23
    Scrambled Eggs with Herbs and Smoked Salmon–Bacon Toast, 239
    Soft Scrambled Eggs, 22
    Tricolor Omelet, 24
    Zucchini and Fresh Goat Cheese Frittata, 28
endives:
    Caramelized Endives, 169
    Endive and Avocado Gazpacho, 65
    Endives *Confites* with Blue Cheese Crostini, 172
    Endive with Green Tomato Jam, 71
    Roasted Chicken with Endives, 217–18
    Salmon with Endives and Oranges *en Papillote,* 160–61
escarole, Bruschetta with Escarole, 221

Farfalle with Yogurt-Basil Sauce, 90
Fargue, Léon Paul, 138
fennel:
    Cod with Fennel and Orange *en Papillote,* 159
    Flounder Fillets with Fennel, 98–99
    Italian-style Fennel and Apple Salad, 75
    Lentil, Fennel, and Orange Salad, 175
    Potato and Fennel Purée, 126
    Roasted Vegetables with Cumin, 166
    Shaved Fennel and Citrus Salad, 74

fennel (*cont.*)
  Shrimp and Fennel Salad, 216
  Smoked Salmon, Fennel, and
    Orange Mille-Feuille, 48–49
fish:
  author's notes on, 91–92, 153–58
  Bouillabaisse Twenty-first
    Century, 96–97
  cooking *en papillote*, 158
  for dinner, 136–44
  for lunch, 91–100
  overcoming resistance to, 156
  recipes, 159–64
  see also specific fish
Fish Day, 225–33
  Apricot Tart, 232–33
  Avocado-Apple Salad with
    Gambas, 227
  Lemon Ricotta Pancakes, 226
  menu, 225
  Red Snapper *en Papillote*, 228
  Scallop "Ceviche" with Mango
    and Parmesan, 230
  Skate *à la Grenobloise*, 231
  Yogurt with *Crème Chocolat*,
    229
Flammekueche, Savory, 53
Flammekueche, Sweet, 54–55
flaxseed oil, 14
Flounder Fillets with Fennel,
  98–99
Flounder Fillets with Paprika
  Sauce, 142–43
French Fries, Sweet Potato, 131
French Toast Edward Style, 57
Fried Eggs, Spanish Style, 25
fried foods, 211
frittatas:
  Ham and Leek Frittata, 27
  Zucchini and Fresh Goat Cheese
    Frittata, 28
Fromage Blanc with Blue Cheese
  and Chives, 51
fruit salads:
  Fruit Salad with Quinoa, 186
  Grated Fruit and Veggie "Slaw,"
    76
  Yogurt and Fruit Salad, 198

Fusilli with Spinach and
  Anchovies, 87

gazpachos:
  Beet and Ginger Gazpacho, 66
  Beet and Zucchini Gazpacho, 67
  Endive and Avocado Gazpacho,
    65
Giovanna's MBC:
  author's notes on, 17, 19
  recipe, 18
Gladwell, Malcolm, 274
globalization, 277
goat cheese:
  Goat Cheese and Hazelnut
    Tartines, 38
  Zucchini and Fresh Goat Cheese
    Frittata, 28
Grandma Louise's Oatmeal with
  Grated Apple, 214
grapefruit:
  Grapefruit, Avocado, and Caviar
    Mille-Feuille, 47
  Shaved Fennel and Citrus Salad,
    74
Grated Fruit and Veggie "Slaw,"
  76
Grissini, Prosciutto Wrapped
  Around, 255

ham:
  Ham and Leek Frittata, 27
  Prosciutto Wrapped around
    Grissini, 255
  Velouté of Haricots Verts with
    Peppers and Ham, 220
Haricots Verts Salad with Peaches
  and Almonds, 78
health issues, 274–76
homemade food, 276–78

ingredients, 279–83
Italian-style Chicken, 148
Italian-style Fennel and Apple
  Salad, 75

John Dory with Tomatoes and
  Capers, 100

Juncker, Madame Berthe, 11–13

kiwi:
  Carrot Soup with Yogurt and
    Kiwi, 70
  Yogurt and Fruit Salad, 198

labels, reading, 263–67
lamb, Rosemary Lamb Meatballs,
  146
L'atelier des Chefs, 277
leeks:
  Ham and Leek Frittata, 27
  Leek and Zucchini Salad, 176
  Leeks and Onion Parmesan, 222
  Leeks Mozzarella, 133
  Mackerel with Carrots and
    Leeks, 137
  Mackerel with Curry and Leeks,
    141
  Magical Leek Broth, 68–69
  Potage d'Hiver (Winter Soup),
    115
  Salmon with Leeks and
    Asparagus *en Papillote*,
    162–63
  Sardines with Carrots and Leeks,
    136
  Tagliatelle with Leeks and
    Prosciutto, 85
lemon:
  Baked Apples with Lemon
    Cream, 253
  Lemon Curd, 202
  Lemon Ricotta Pancakes, 226
  Lemon Toasts, 52
  Oatmeal with Lemon Zest and
    Prunes, 30
  Potato Ragoût with Peppers,
    Lemon, and Olives, 129
  Spaghetti *al Limone*, 88
Lentil, Fennel, and Orange Salad,
  175
Lentil and Celeriac Soup, 116
Light Work Day, 219–24
  Bruschetta with Escarole, 221
  Leeks and Onion Parmesan, 222
  menu, 219

Roasted *Daurade* (Sea Bream), with Vegetables, 223

Tarte au Chocolat, 224

Velouté of Haricots Verts with Peppers and Ham, 220

lime, Spaghetti with Lime and Arugula, 89

Linguine with Shrimp, Tomatoes, and Basil, 86

lunch, 59–106

  author's notes on, 61–64

  fish, 91–100

  meat, 101–6

  pasta, 83–90

  salads, 71–76

  soups, 65–70

  vegetable dishes, 77–82

Macaroni with Ricotta and Walnuts, 124

Mâche, Celeriac, and Beet Salad, 72

Mackerel with Carrots and Leeks, 137

Mackerel with Curry and Leeks, 141

Madeleines au Chocolat, 204–5

Magical Breakfast Cream:

  author's notes on, 11–14

  Giovanna's variation, 18; notes, 17, 19

  options, tips, and tricks, 16–17

  recipe, 15

Magical Leek Broth, 68–69

mango:

  Mango Lassi, the French Way, 196

  Scallop "Ceviche" with Mango and Parmesan, 230

meats:

  for dinner, 145–50

  for lunch, 101–6

menus:

  Brunch for 4 or 8, 238

  Champagne Medley Dinner, 254

  Chicken *Tout au Champagne*, 249

  Fish Day, 225

  Light Work Day, 219

  Ordinary Day, 213

  Valentine's Day Dinner, 234

Milk Jam (*Confiture de Lait*), 45

mille-feuille:

  Cheese-Apple Mille-Feuille, 50

  Grapefruit, Avocado, and Caviar Mille-Feuille, 47

  Smoked Salmon, Fennel, and Orange Mille-Feuille, 48–49

monkfish, Steamed Monkfish with Vegetables, 93

mozzarella, Leeks Mozzarella, 133

mushrooms:

  Crimini Salad, 82

  Mushrooms and Swiss Chard, 132

  Poêlée of Mushrooms, 250

  Provençal Omelet, 23

  Tilapia with Cumin and Mushrooms, 94

nuts:

  Apple Compote with Pistachios, 184

  Cream of Wheat with Cranberries and Walnuts, 34

  Goat Cheese and Hazelnut *Tartines*, 38

  Haricots Verts Salad with Peaches and Almonds, 78

  Macaroni with Ricotta and Walnuts, 124

  Quinoa with Almonds, Hazelnuts, and Apricots, 33

  Yogurt and Fruit Salad, 198

  Yogurt and Nut "Cocktail," 197

oatmeal:

  Grandma Louise's Oatmeal with Grated Apple, 214

  Oatmeal with Lemon Zest and Prunes, 30

  Peanut Butter Banana Oatmeal, 31

  Strawberry-Banana Oatmeal Smoothie, 32

  Yogurt and Oatmeal Cake, 199

Obama, Michelle, 256

omelets:

  Provençal Omelet, 23

  Tricolor Omelet, 24

onions:

  Leeks and Onion Parmesan, 222

  Onion *Poêlée* with Apples, 173

  Roasted Vegetables with Cumin, 166

  Vegetable Curry, 165

oranges:

  Carrot and Orange Soup, 215

  Cod with Fennel and Orange *en Papillote*, 159

  Lentil, Fennel, and Orange Salad, 175

  Salmon with Endives and Oranges *en Papillote*, 160–61

  Shaved Fennel and Citrus Salad, 74

  Smoked Salmon, Fennel, and Orange Mille-Feuille, 48–49

Ordinary Day, 213–18

  Carrot and Orange Soup, 215

  Grandma Louise's Oatmeal with Grated Apple, 214

  menu, 213

  Roasted Chicken with Endives, 217–18

  Shrimp and Fennel Salad, 216

Orecchiette with Broccoli Rabe and Sausage, 119

organic foods, 278–79

Oysters, Fried, 138–39

pancakes:

  Caramelized Chicken with Vegetable "Pancake," 104–5

  Lemon Ricotta Pancakes, 226

Panna Cotta, 200–201

Parmesan:

  Clafoutis Provençal, 46

  Cucumber, Prosciutto, and Parmesan *Tartines*, 40

  Leeks and Onion Parmesan, 222

  Parmesan Polenta with Prosciutto, 44

  Provençal Omelet, 23

Parmesan (*cont.*)
  Scallop "Ceviche" with Mango
    and Parmesan, 230
  Spaghetti *al Limone*, 88
  Spaghetti Carbonara, 120–21
  Spaghetti Carbonara *alla
    Edoardo*, 122–23
  Spaghetti with Lime and
    Arugula, 89
parsnips, Carrot Parsnip Purée, 174
pasta:
  author's notes on, 83
  dinner, 119–25
  Farfalle with Yogurt-Basil Sauce,
    90
  Fusilli with Spinach and
    Anchovies, 87
  Linguine with Shrimp,
    Tomatoes, and Basil, 86
  lunch, 83–90
  Macaroni with Ricotta and
    Walnuts, 124
  Orecchiette with Broccoli Rabe
    and Sausage, 119
  Penne with Eggplant and Tuna, 84
  Spaghetti *al Limone*, 88
  Spaghetti Carbonara, 120–21
  Spaghetti Carbonara *alla
    Edoardo*, 122–23
  Spaghetti with Lime and
    Arugula, 89
  Tagliatelle with Leeks and
    Prosciutto, 85
  Tagliatelle with Turkey
    "Bolognese," 125
peaches:
  Haricots Verts Salad with
    Peaches and Almonds, 78
  Yogurt and Fruit Salad, 198
Peanut Butter Banana Oatmeal, 31
pears:
  Cream of Celeriac with Pear and
    Blue Cheese, 118
  Duck Breasts with Pears, 257
  Pear and Blue Cheese *Tartines*,
    42
  Pear and Date au Gratin, 185
  Yogurt and Fruit Salad, 198

peas:
  Quinoa with Peas and Favas, 127
  Sauté of Peas and Prosciutto with
    Fresh Mint, 77
Penne with Eggplant and Tuna, 84
peppers:
  Poêlée Provençale, 168
  Potato Ragoût with Peppers,
    Lemon, and Olives, 129
  Velouté of Haricots Verts with
    Peppers and Ham, 220
Pineapple, Yogurt, and Chocolate
  Verrines, 192
pistachios:
  Apple Compote with Pistachios,
    184
  Yogurt and Fruit Salad, 198
Poached Eggs with Salmon and
  Spinach, 26
Poêlée of Mushrooms, 250
Poêlée Provençale, 168
polenta, Parmesan Polenta with
  Prosciutto, 44
Pork Chops with Apples, 145
portion control, 62–63, 64, 182
Potage d'Hiver (Winter Soup), 115
potatoes:
  Black Olive Potato Salad with
    Fava Beans, 135
  Potage d'Hiver (Winter Soup),
    115
  Potato and Fennel Purée, 126
  Potato Ragoût with Peppers,
    Lemon, and Olives, 129
  Skate *à la Grenobloise*, 231
  Vegetable Curry, 165
prosciutto:
  Cucumber, Prosciutto, and
    Parmesan *Tartines*, 40
  Parmesan Polenta with
    Prosciutto, 44
  Prosciutto Wrapped Around
    Grissini, 255
  Sauté of Peas and Prosciutto with
    Fresh Mint, 77
  Tagliatelle with Leeks and
    Prosciutto, 85
Provençal Omelet, 23

prunes, Oatmeal with Lemon Zest
  and Prunes, 30
pumpkin:
  Pumpkin and Apple Gratin, 167
  Pumpkin and Apple Soup, 117
  Roasted Carrots and Pumpkin
    with Herbs, 130
putting it all together, 207–40
  author's notes on, 209–12
  Brunch for 4 or 8, 238–40
  Fish Day, 225–33
  Light Work Day, 219–24
  Ordinary Day, 213–18
  Valentine's Day Dinner, 234–38

quinoa:
  Fruit Salad with Quinoa, 186
  Quinoa and Beet Salad, 134
  Quinoa with Almonds,
    Hazelnuts, and Apricots, 33
  Quinoa with Peas and Favas,
    127

ragoût, Potato Ragoût with
    Peppers, Lemon, and Olives,
    129
Raspberry-Banana Smoothie, 189
Raspberry-Blackberry Rice
    Pudding Verrines, 191
Ratatouille, 80–81
Red Berry Smoothie, 188
Red Snapper *en Papillote*, 228
Rhubarb Smoothie, 190
ricotta:
  Lemon Ricotta Pancakes, 226
  Macaroni with Ricotta and
    Walnuts, 124
  Ricotta and Anchovy *Tartines*,
    39
Ripert, Eric, Croque Monsieur
    Eric Ripert Style, 56
Rosemary Lamb Meatballs, 146

salads:
  Black Olive Potato Salad with
    Fava Beans, 135
  Carrot and Celeriac Salad, 73
  Crimini Salad, 82

Endive with Green Tomato Jam, 71

Fruit Salad with Quinoa, 186

Grated Fruit and Veggie "Slaw," 76

Haricots Verts Salad with Peaches and Almonds, 78

Italian-style Fennel and Apple Salad, 75

Leek and Zucchini Salad, 176

Lentil, Fennel, and Orange Salad, 175

lunch, 71–76

Mâche, Celeriac, and Beet Salad, 72

Quinoa and Beet Salad, 134

Shaved Fennel and Citrus Salad, 74

Shrimp and Fennel Salad, 216

Sweet-and-Sour Carrot Salad, 177

Yogurt and Fruit Salad, 198

salmon:

Croque Monsieur Eric Ripert Style, 56

Poached Eggs with Salmon and Spinach, 26

Salmon with Endives and Oranges en Papillote, 160–61

Salmon with Leeks and Asparagus en Papillote, 162–63

Scrambled Eggs with Herbs and Smoked Salmon–Bacon Toast, 239

Smoked Salmon, Fennel, and Orange Mille-Feuille, 48–49

salsa, Sea Bass with Celeriac-Mint Salsa, 95

salt, 211, 266

sandwiches:

Croque Monsieur Eric Ripert Style, 56

Mushrooms and Swiss Chard, 132

sardines:

Sardines with Carrots and Leeks, 136

Sardine Tartines, 41

sauces, dessert:

Baked Apples with Lemon Cream, 253

Yogurt with Crème Chocolat, 229

sauces, savory:

Paprika Sauce, 142–43

Quick "Aïoli," 140

Tuna with Green Sauce, 144

Yogurt-Basil Sauce, 90

sausage:

Fried Eggs, Spanish Style, 25

Orecchiette with Broccoli Rabe and Sausage, 119

Savory Flammekueche, 53

Scallop "Ceviche" with Mango and Parmesan, 230

Scallops Maison Blanche, 256

Scrambled Eggs, Soft, 22

Scrambled Eggs with Herbs and Smoked Salmon–Bacon Toast, 239

Sea Bass with Celeriac-Mint Salsa, 95

Sea Bass with Sweet Spices en Papillote, 164

sea bream, Roasted Daurade (Sea Bream) with Vegetables, 223

Sea Scallop and Fleur de Sel Tartines, 43

shrimp:

Avocado-Apple Salad with Gambas, 227

Linguine with Shrimp, Tomatoes, and Basil, 86

Shrimp and Fennel Salad, 216

Skate à la Grenobloise, 231

smoothies, 187–94

author's notes on, 187

Raspberry-Banana Smoothie, 189

Red Berry Smoothie, 188

Rhubarb Smoothie, 190

Strawberry-Banana Oatmeal Smoothie, 32

Soft Scrambled Eggs, 22

Sondheim, Stephen, 210

soups:

author's notes on, 63–64, 211–12

Bouillabaisse Twenty-first Century, 96–97

Butternut Squash Soup, 114

Carrot and Orange Soup, 215

Carrot Soup with Yogurt and Kiwi, 70

Cream of Celeriac with Pear and Blue Cheese, 118

dinner, 114–18

Endive and Avocado Gazpacho, 65

Lentil and Celeriac Soup, 116

lunch, 65–70

Magical Leek Broth, 68–69

Potage d'Hiver (Winter Soup), 115

Pumpkin and Apple Soup, 117

Velouté of Haricots Verts with Peppers and Ham, 220

spaghetti:

Spaghetti al Limone, 88

Spaghetti Carbonara, 120–21

Spaghetti Carbonara alla Edoardo, 122–23

Spaghetti with Lime and Arugula, 89

Spanish Style Fried Eggs, 25

Spiced Chocolate Mousse, 206

spinach:

Chicken with Spinach en Papillote, 103

Fusilli with Spinach and Anchovies, 87

Poached Eggs with Salmon and Spinach, 26

Provençal Omelet, 23

Scallops Maison Blanche, 256

Strawberry-Banana Oatmeal Smoothie, 32

Strawberry Parfait, 258

Sweet-and-Sour Carrot Salad, 177

Sweet Flammekueche, 54–55

sweet potatoes:

Carrot Parsnip Purée, 174

Sweet Potato French Fries, 131

Swiss chard, Mushrooms and Swiss Chard, 132

Tagliatelle with Leeks and Prosciutto, 85

Tagliatelle with Turkey
  "Bolognese," 125
Tarte au Chocolat, 224
tartines:
  author's notes on, 36–37
  Crab *Tartines* Avocado, 240
  Cucumber, Prosciutto, and
    Parmesan *Tartines,* 40
  Goat Cheese and Hazelnut
    Tartines, 38
  Parmesan Polenta with
    Prosciutto, 44
  Pear and Blue Cheese *Tartines,*
    42
  Ricotta and Anchovy *Tartines,* 39
  Sardine *Tartines,* 41
  Sea Scallop and Fleur de Sel
    Tartines, 43
teaching new habits, 271–74
Tilapia with Cumin and
    Mushrooms, 94
tomatoes:
  Endive with Green Tomato Jam,
    71
  John Dory with Tomatoes and
    Capers, 100
  Linguine with Shrimp,
    Tomatoes, and Basil, 86
  Provençal Omelet, 23
  Ratatouille, 80–81
  Stuffed Zucchini, 252
Tricolor Omelet, 24
tuna:
  Penne with Eggplant and Tuna,
    84
  Tuna with Green Sauce, 144
turkey:
  Sauté of Turkey with Spring
    Vegetables, 102

Tagliatelle with Turkey
  "Bolognese," 125
turnips, Roasted Vegetables with
    Cumin, 166

Valentine's Day Dinner, 234–38
  Classic Chocolate Mousse,
    236–37
  Duck Breasts *à la Gasconne* with
    Wild Rice, 235
  menu, 234
Veal Scaloppine *à la Moutarde,* 101
vegetables:
  author's notes on, 153–58
  Caramelized Chicken with
    Vegetable "Pancake," 104–5
  for dinner, 126–35
  for lunch, 77–82
  overcoming resistance to, 156–57
  raw, 211
  recipes, 165–77
  Roasted *Daurade* (Sea Bream)
    with Vegetables, 223
  Roasted Vegetables with Cumin,
    166
  Sauté of Turkey with Spring
    Vegetables, 102
  Steamed Monkfish with
    Vegetables, 93
  Vegetable Curry, 165
  see also specific vegetables
Velouté of Haricots Verts with
    Peppers and Ham, 220
verrines:
  author's notes on, 187
  Chocolate-Coffee Verrines,
    193
  Pineapple, Yogurt, and
    Chocolate Verrines, 192

Raspberry-Blackberry Rice
    Pudding Verrines, 191

walking, 268
walnuts:
  Cream of Wheat with
    Cranberries and Walnuts, 34
  Macaroni with Ricotta and
    Walnuts, 124
water, drinking, 267–68
wild rice, Duck Breasts *à la
    Gasconne* with Wild Rice, 235

yogurt, 266–67
  Asparagus with Yogurt Dressing,
    79
  Carrot Soup with Yogurt and
    Kiwi, 70
  Farfalle with Yogurt-Basil Sauce,
    90
  Giovanna's MBC, 18
  Magical Breakfast Cream, 15
  Pineapple, Yogurt, and
    Chocolate Verrines, 192
  Strawberry Parfait, 258
  Yogurt and Fruit Salad, 198
  Yogurt and Nut "Cocktail," 197
  Yogurt and Oatmeal Cake, 199
  Yogurt with *Crème Chocolat,* 229

zucchini:
  Beet and Zucchini Gazpacho, 67
  Leek and Zucchini Salad, 176
  Poêlée Provençale, 168
  Ratatouille, 80–81
  Stuffed Zucchini, 252
  Vegetable Curry, 165
  Zucchini and Fresh Goat Cheese
    Frittata, 28